IN THE
MIND'S EYE

*'If I were to look out west I would see ... a few lights
flickering from Bideford ... like coloured stars on a cold night.
A friend tells me I can't see them, but he is wrong, for in
my mind I see things well. They blaze sometimes.'*

**Colonel Sir Mike Ansell, (1906–1994),
President of St Dunstan's (1977–1986).**

IN THE MIND'S EYE

The Blinded Veterans of St Dunstan's

(As Blind Veterans UK, the charity now cares for
ex-servicepeople blind from any cause)

David Castleton

Pen & Sword
MILITARY

First published in Great Britain by
PEN AND SWORD MILITARY
an imprint of
Pen and Sword Books Ltd
47 Church Street
Barnsley
South Yorkshire S70 2AS

Copyright © David Castleton, 2013

ISBN 978 1 78159 347 9

The right of David Castleton to be identified
as the author of this work has been asserted by him
in accordance with the Copyright, Designs and Patents Act 1988.

A CIP record for this book is available from the British Library.

Printed and bound in England by
CPI Group (UK) Ltd, Croydon, CR0 4YY

Typeset in Times by CHIC GRAPHICS

Pen & Sword Books Ltd incorporates the imprints of
Pen & Sword Aviation, Pen & Sword Family History, Pen & Sword Maritime,
Pen & Sword Military, Pen & Sword Discovery, Wharncliffe Local History,
Wharncliffe True Crime, Wharncliffe Transport, Pen & Sword Select,
Pen & Sword Military Classics, Leo Cooper, Remember When,
The Praetorian Press, Seaforth Publishing and Frontline Publishing

For a complete list of Pen and Sword titles please contact
Pen and Sword Books Limited
47 Church Street, Barnsley, South Yorkshire, S70 2AS, England
E-mail: enquiries@pen-and-sword.co.uk
Website: www.pen-and-sword.co.uk

Contents

Foreword

It is a great privilege for me, as Chief Executive of Blind Veterans UK (St Dunstan's since 1915), to have been asked to write a foreword for David Castleton's history of the formative years of this unique and very special organisation. It is the feeling, which both members and staff have, of being part of the 'family' of Blind Veterans UK that is a major component of the life-changing difference that we are able to make for ex-service men and women who thought their loss of sight was the end of their useful lives.

This life-changing experience is encapsulated by a recurring theme I pick up from our members and it always goes something like this: "I was lonely and afraid as I lost my sight. Suddenly, I couldn't do any of the things for myself that I had always taken for granted. I couldn't drive my car any more, I couldn't read a newspaper, I couldn't watch television, I couldn't deal with my own correspondence. I couldn't even get to the local shop on my own. I was effectively becoming a prisoner in my own home. Then Blind Veterans UK threw me a lifeline".

From the trenches of the Somme to the deserts of Afghanistan that lifeline has been making an extraordinary difference to the lives of blind ex-service men and women for almost a hundred years. This organisation has a great and glorious past, from its foundation by a blind man of vision, and it is for those of us who come after to carry the torch that he lit all those years ago, into a great and glorious future.

As the organisation goes forward, celebrating its past as St Dunstan's and its future as Blind Veterans UK, I am confident that it will be a beacon in the darkness for more and more ex-service men and women, helping them to discover that there is a life beyond sight loss and that none of them has to battle their blindness alone.

David Castleton has been associated with this organisation for many years, both as a long-serving member of staff and now as a volunteer. I am hugely grateful to him for using his encyclopaedic knowledge and long experience to chronicle our remarkable story.

Robert Leader,
CEO of Blind Veterans UK, January 2013.

Prologue

This book began as an account of the early years of St Dunstan's from its foundation in 1915, but it soon became clear that behind the facts and figures, behind the politics, is a story of the contribution made by war-blinded men and women to an organisation founded by a blind man. This is not just the fact that, by their successful rehabilitation into the everyday life of this country, war-blinded St Dunstaners set an example to blind people and charities working for them. It is also the contribution made by many to the working of the organisation that had helped them.

Numerous St Dunstaners have taught others the skills they had learned. When the Second World War began, men blinded in the First World War returned to St Dunstan's not only to teach, but also to inspire the next generation by their ability to overcome the handicap they shared. Others used their talents to help raise the funds needed to keep the work going, while a few headed specialist departments and contributed to the committees that directed St Dunstan's work.

With the approval of the Charity Commission, St Dunstan's has widened its work to include all ex-service people who have lost their sight through causes other than actual service in war. The organisation has embarked on this new task with greatly increasing numbers of blind ex-service men and women and a pressing need for funds to expand its facilities for training. With this in mind, in February 2012 a decision was taken, after much research, to change the name of the charity to Blind Veterans UK. This is to appeal, in both senses of the word, to younger generations for whom the title St Dunstan's has failed to convey the nature of its work.

This is a good time to record those early days, and in doing so remind the sighted community of the existence of Blind Veterans UK and its continuing responsibility for the welfare of blind ex-service people. At the same time, apart from casualties from Iraq and Afghanistan, the number of war-blinded men and women has inevitably been decreasing since the Second World War. This account is a tribute to the courage and tenacity of ordinary men and women in overcoming the trauma of blindness in two world wars and the example they have set for all those who lose their sight in war or peace.

David Castleton, 2013.

Chapter 1

Pearson's Vision

"I will never be a blind man, I will be the blind man!"
(Sir Arthur Pearson, 1913)

T ommy Milligan, a young assistant pastry cook, lived in Roundhill
Street, just off the Albert Bridge Road in Belfast. Like many of his
contemporaries Tommy looked to the British Army as a means of
opportunity and on 28 May 1914 he celebrated his eighteenth birthday by
enlisting in the Irish Guards. Within three months the First World War was
declared and soon Tommy was serving in France with his regiment. During
action at La Bassee in December 1914, Tommy was wounded and totally
blinded. His short military career ended, he was among a convoy of injured
men sailing from France to Cardiff.

A Cardiff newspaper reported the presence of a blind man among the
casualties. Although, as the war ground on some 2,000 young men would
lose their sight, in those early months a blinded soldier was news. That
article was fortunate for young Tommy, as it brought a number of volunteers
to the military hospital with offers of help. Among them was the daughter
of a wealthy Cardiff shipbroker, a 17-year-old girl whose own sight was in
danger and who had been taught Braille in consequence. The medical officer
arranged for her to give Tommy Milligan some preliminary Braille lessons,
and these gave Tommy his first hope that he might be able to tackle the
handicap of blindness. More than this, through her father, she brought
Tommy into contact with the man who would show him how that handicap
could be overcome.

On 29 January 1915, in London at York House, St James's Palace, Mr
C. Arthur Pearson, President of the National Institute for the Blind, and
himself blind, had called a meeting to establish the Blinded Soldiers and

1

Sailors Care Committee. The Cardiff shipbroker, an acquaintance of Arthur Pearson, was aware of the new committee and told Pearson about Tommy Milligan. Pearson travelled to Cardiff and took Tommy back to London, where he became one of the first members of a 'regiment' of young, blinded soldiers who were to pioneer Pearson's progressive ideas for training blind people. In fact, if early records can be trusted, Tommy was probably the second St Dunstaner, his entry being dated 11 February 1915. The first was John Batchelor of the 3rd Royal Sussex Regiment, who was admitted one day before Tommy. John Batchelor was a regular soldier and had already served for six years before he was wounded at Ypres in October 1914. He would go on to train as a mat-maker at St Dunstan's.

John and Tommy's rescuer was no ordinary blind man. Arthur Pearson was born in 1866 at Wookey in Somerset, the son of the Reverend Arthur Cyril Pearson, who was at that time a curate. Pearson was educated at Eagle House, Wimbledon and, for a short time, at Winchester College, which he subsequently described in his forthright way as 'a waste of time and money'. A competition in George Newnes's *Tit-Bits* magazine led to his entry into journalism. The prize was a job on the staff of *Tit-Bits* at £100 a year. Pearson won it by dint of frequently cycling the 40-mile round trip to his nearest reference library to find the answers to ten questions that appeared in the magazine each week.

The magazine's management must have been somewhat shaken when the winner turned out to be just 18 years old, but they kept their word and engaged him. The energy Pearson had showed in winning the competition he also brought to his new career and by the time he was 19 Pearson was already manager and George Newnes's right-hand man. Later Pearson left Newnes to set up his own magazine *Pearson's Weekly* and, building on that success, he went on to found the *Daily Express* in 1900. In 1904 he added the *Evening Standard* to what had become the Pearson publishing empire.

For the most part of his journalistic career – and he was a 'hands-on' proprietor, editing the *Express* himself – Pearson did not take up any strong political position. However, in 1901 he became convinced of the need for Britain to give up its free trade policy. Through the columns of his newspapers he urged tariff reform, the imposition of tariffs on imports to protect industries at home and from the British Empire. This brought him into contact with Joseph Chamberlain, who was advocating tariff reform in Parliament, and he became one of Chamberlain's strongest supporters. Ironically in later years Chamberlain's son Neville would prove himself less than sympathetic to Pearson's son, also Neville, when St Dunstan's came under criticism.

Significantly, Pearson also turned to charitable work by establishing the Pearson Fresh Air Fund in 1892 to provide days out in the country for poor city children. He proved to be as successful in fundraising as he was in publishing. Early on in the First World War Pearson was appointed joint honorary secretary of the Collection Committee of the Prince of Wales Fund. This later became the National Relief Fund, a source of assistance for the newly founded Blinded Soldiers and Sailors Hostel.

Pearson's change of course from newspaper proprietor to political campaigner began on 18 March 1908, when he was operated on for glaucoma. After the operation he was never able to see well enough to read or write. In 1913, with his sight deteriorating, a specialist advised Pearson to give up his business interests. Facing the fact that he would soon be blind, he told his wife, "I will never be *a* blind man, I am going to be *the* blind man". Boastful? No, his contribution to blind welfare would turn out to be ample justification for his confidence. He applied to himself, and to the young blind men who were to come into his care, his own code: "To be blind may mean to be helpless, incompetent, perpetually resigned to a life of dull ineptitude. To be blind may mean to carry on one's life almost as before, to put up with minor inconvenience in conquering problems as they present themselves. Lots of people see without perceiving, blind people learn to perceive without seeing".

This was the man Tommy Milligan set off with on the journey to London. "I had great trust in him", recalled Tommy, "because I had often read *Pearson's Weekly* and I knew he was a man of distinction. He was a man who inspired confidence as soon as you met him and you knew he was an organiser – a man who could grasp a situation quickly and deal with it. He told me about his blindness going up in the train". Tommy Milligan's words sum up Pearson's unique assets in reshaping the lives of so many young men facing the trauma of blindness. He was famous, he inspired confidence, and above all he too was blind. Arthur Pearson was to become a legend for a generation of blinded ex-servicemen.

Chapter 2

Regent's Park and Rehabilitation

"Once again I was a useful member of society,"
(Tommy Rogers, St Dunstaner)

Pearson soon had the opportunity to fulfil the ambition he had set himself to become '*the* blind man'. As early as February 1912 he was invited to join the Council of the British and Foreign Blind Association. He accepted in October 1913, and became Treasurer in January 1914. Publicist as he was, Pearson's next aim was to change the name of the organisation to something more prestigious. His successful fundraising efforts provided money for a new headquarters in Great Portland Street and the British and Foreign Blind Association became the National Institute for the Blind, just before His Majesty King George V and Queen Mary formally opened the building. Pearson's reward was unanimous election to the presidency of the Institute by a grateful committee.

After the outbreak of war in July 1914, at a meeting on 8 September the council resolved that 'steps should be taken to make it known that the Institute would, as far as practicable, help such men as lose their sight whilst on service in the war'. The way in which this should be done was left to Pearson, as the President/Treasurer, and Mr Henry Stainsby, the Secretary-General. Pearson did not neglect his duty, and by early December 1914 he was in touch with all British military hospitals, tracing eye casualties. He knew of nine British and two Belgian blinded soldiers in hospital at that time. Ever the practical man, Pearson had also appealed to the Select Committee on Naval and Military Pensions, pressing the claims of these first few blinded soldiers and had received acknowledgement from David

4

Lloyd George and encouraging replies from other members of the committee.

By January 1915 Pearson had discovered 22 blinded soldiers. "All require to be promptly and sympathetically dealt with", he explained to the Blinded Soldiers and Sailors Care Committee. "They should be taught to read and write in the embossed type, assisted to acquire some occupation and generally trained to become active, self-reliant and self-helpful". It would be the object of the committee to establish a convalescent home equipped and maintained for such training.

Pearson arranged for all of these war-blinded men to be transferred to the Second London General Hospital at St Marks College, Chelsea. This was not far from 6 Bayswater Road, a large private house loaned for use as a military hospital and where the first six of Pearson's protégés were housed. Work began there, but on a temporary basis, because Pearson had already received a magnificent offer that would satisfy his specification for an ideal training centre: "For my hostel I had the idea of a place with plenty of room to move about and with large and beautiful grounds. I wanted delightful surroundings. Directly or indirectly surroundings have their influence on the blind. Moreover I wanted to find these desirable conditions in a central part of London". There cannot be many places in London more central than Regent's Park and it was here that Pearson was offered St Dunstan's Villa, a house with 15 acres of grounds for his hostel. The estate was loaned with blanket permission to erect temporary buildings necessary to establish workshops and classrooms.

Surprisingly Pearson's benefactor was German-born Otto Kahn, an Anglophile who spoke with an English accent, had his suits made in Savile Row and had become a naturalised English citizen. He had moved to London from Mannheim to work for Deutsche Bank and was regarded as a successful financier. Kahn was also interested in the arts and was popular among London's smart set, attending parties where the Prince of Wales (later King Edward VIII), whom he was said to resemble, was often a guest.

Otto Kahn had not long purchased St Dunstan's Villa from Lord Londesborough when war broke out. His unconditional offer of its use gave Pearson's project a flying start – and a name. St Dunstan's Villa had been named for a large clock set up in the grounds, which had originally embellished the church of St Dunstan-in-the-West, in Fleet Street. When it was installed in 1671 it was the first public clock in London to have a minute hand. Over the years it became something of an attraction, as people would gather in Fleet Street to see its two giants, Gog and Magog, mark the hours by striking a bell with their pole-axes.

Among the sightseers in the early part of the nineteenth century was a small boy who grew up to become the Marquess of Hertford. In 1830 the Marquess had the opportunity to acquire the clock that had fascinated him as a boy. When the Church of St Dunstan-in-the-West fell on hard times, the Marquess of Hertford bought the clock at auction. He had it set up in the grounds of the house he was building in Regent's Park and named his house St Dunstan's Villa. In 1935, long after St Dunstan's headquarters had moved elsewhere, Lord Rothermere, another newspaper proprietor, bought the property and returned the clock and its giants to their rightful home on the church in Fleet Street.

Although the organisation would later be separated from the house and clock, the name they bestowed was now irrevocably settled upon it. Between the two world wars St Dunstan's became one of the most famous names in the field of welfare of blind people. In popular vernacular it became symbolic of blindness – a sports team that won by an unusually large score would be asked, "Were you playing St Dunstan's?" Many came to believe, erroneously, that St Dunstan was the patron saint of blind people. So soon was the name officially accepted that Pearson's first annual report in March 1916 bore the title 'Report of St Dunstan's Hostel for Blinded Soldiers and Sailors'. It recorded proudly that the hostel had already been visited by, 'The King and Queen, Queen Alexandra, The Prince of Wales, Princess Victoria and other members of the Royal Family', as well as many other high profile public figures.

On the cover of the report was a drawing showing a handsome, young blinded soldier being led by a small girl holding his hand. Versions of this illustration became powerful symbols used on emblems sold on St Dunstan's flag days. But this was not merely a fundraising invention. The small girl really existed and was in the habit of leading blinded men around the grounds of the hostel. Her name was Ruby Smith, and she was the daughter of the head gardener of the estate, who was still employed by Otto Kahn to look after the grounds while St Dunstan's was in occupation. Little Ruby, as she became known, had the run of the grounds and soon she was befriending St Dunstaners. From the age of three to nine, Ruby grew up as the only child among a community of young blinded men and their sighted instructors and helpers.

Many years later, now Mrs Ruby Crane, a widow in retirement, she recalled some of her childhood memories of the coming of St Dunstan's Hostel: "I remember horses and carts bringing in stuff. When they were putting up wooden buildings they padded the posts and supports with straw with red felt wound round. There were handrails everywhere to everything. Although the buildings were all over the lawns my father realised it was all in a good cause". Young as she was, Ruby understood that the young men who now filled her world could not see. "I used to go up to them and chat and we'd walk around just holding hands. If they wanted to go to a certain workshop I knew them all by heart. I always remember how my little hand seemed so small in theirs".

Ruby made a weekly visit to Arthur Pearson, taking him roses from her father. It was a small ceremony that the 'Chief', as he became known to St Dunstaners, clearly enjoyed. Among her cherished mementos of those days is a letter from Pearson, written to his six-year-old supporter in 1918: 'Dear Little Ruby, The collecting box you brought me yesterday had 18s 3d in it. I think it is very sweet of you to collect this for the blinded soldiers. Yours sincerely, Arthur Pearson'.

* * * * *

On 26 March 1916, the same day that the first annual report was published, 14 blinded soldiers moved into the new hostel in Regent's Park. By then Pearson had become a father figure to 150 trainees at the hostel or in annexes established in London, Brighton and Torquay, including five Australians, two New Zealanders and seven Canadians.

Two-thirds of St Dunstaners admitted were totally blind and the great majority of the remaining third could only distinguish light from dark. A small minority, about seven per cent, had a small amount of vision but no useful sight. From the beginning the definition of blindness for admission to St Dunstan's was (and still is for Blind Veterans UK), the inability to read, write, or undertake any activity where sight is necessary.

The first steps in rehabilitation began even before a blinded soldier came to Regent's Park. At the Second London General Hospital a blinded casualty was visited as soon as possible, often by Pearson himself, and given a Braille watch. By feeling the strengthened hands and the raised dots indicating the numbers one to twelve, the ability to tell the time independently once more was an important psychological first step to realising that blindness was not a total disaster. After that patients were visited each day and given lessons in Braille and simple hobby occupations to ward off boredom and depression.

Once at Regent's Park they found a carefully prepared and varied training programme. Miss Ethel W. Austin, a member of the Care Committee and Secretary of the National Library for the Blind, began the organisation of teaching reading and writing Braille. This is the first timetable she set for St Dunstaners:

10am-12pm: lessons
12pm-1pm: exercise (walks etc.)
1pm-2pm: dinner
2pm-3pm: newspapers, talk
3pm-5pm: visitors and walks
5pm-5.30pm: tea
5.30pm-6.30pm: lessons
6.30pm-7.30pm: smoker
7.30pm: supper
10pm: lights out.

The basics of training were Braille and typewriting. Braille teachers were drawn from the ranks of voluntary transcribers working for the National Library for the Blind. Braille was not the first system of embossed writing for blind people. However, Louis Braille's invention in 1829 was much less bulky than its predecessors. As a young, blind student, Braille adapted a French Army code using raised dots. There are six in all, arranged like the number six in dominoes. Different numbers and combinations of dots in this pattern signify letters of the alphabet and numbers. The cell of dots is small enough to be covered by the finger tip.

Teaching was on a one-to-one basis and there were as many as 72 teachers in the Braille and typewriting departments, most of them volunteers. Grace Hollins, then Sister Stacey joined them in 1919: "In the Braille room there was a number of instructors at different tables. People came in so many mornings or afternoons a week and had their own pupils", she recalled. Lessons were short and tailored to meet pupils' needs. "You could do this as you liked. I mean, if a man was fussing you didn't make it worse if you could help. I taught the same way as I learnt myself: showing the foundation of six dots. With a machine you wrote opposite to what you read [*Braille writers at that time embossed from the back of the paper*]. They had to pass exams to get their machines. The reading one wasn't so bad – writing was the difficult one".

The value of using blind teachers was quickly recognised. As Pearson put it, 'The remarkable speed with which the occupations taught in the workshops are acquired...is attributable principally to the influence of the blind teacher. The feeling of helplessness which overwhelms a strong, healthy newly blinded man is incredibly relieved when he finds that the one who is to instruct him in some profitable employment is suffering from the same handicap as himself'.

Soon able pupils nearing the end of their own training were employed in teaching their comrades. One of these was Tommy Rogers, who went on to become an employee of St Dunstan's for 26 years. Tommy found in teaching typewriting to others an escape from the frustrations he felt with his own blindness: "I had helped some of the fresh trainees to type their own letters with the result that when a new typing teacher was required the post was offered to me. I accepted and with that acceptance the light began to disperse the mist of frustration. Once again I was a useful member of society".

By 1916, 51 St Dunstaners had already completed training in boot repairing, mat-making, basket-making, joinery, poultry farming, market gardening and, in one case, as a masseur. There were by this time eight men in training to become masseurs, and one of them was the young Irish Guardsman Tommy Milligan who began this story. They were learning an occupation that Pearson regarded as likely to be "the most lucrative of the occupations taught by St Dunstan's".

Other men preferred the idea of a life on the land. For poultry farmers and smallholders, Pearson envisaged setting up each man in a cottage with an acre or so of land and ensuring that he was 'looked after and kept going'. Most poultry farmers were married men, and so, Pearson explained "we endeavour as often as possible to get the wives along and give them two or three weeks' instruction so that they will be able to help their husbands". However, he also recognised that there were limits for blind men in agricultural occupations: "I do not say intensive culture; I think that is rather outside the capabilities of a blind man. We think we have rightly chosen poultry farming and quite simple market gardening, the growing of ordinary vegetables and fruit. There is no doubt at all that if a man follows out the instruction which is given to him at St Dunstan's, he can do fairly well at first and a bit later he ought to do quite well".

Under Pearson's direction, St Dunstan's also experimented with entirely new careers, not previously undertaken by blinded people. Joinery had not been a traditional craft for blind people and the course at St Dunstan's was one of Pearson's innovations. In his realistic way he would not talk of carpentry, "because it is not to be expected that a blind man can become an expert general carpenter unless he was an expert general carpenter before he lost his sight". Rather St Dunstaners were taught to specialise in making about a half a dozen useful and saleable articles under a blind principal instructor, Mr Atkinson, who had been a skilled carpenter before he became blind.

Eventually, about 60 per cent of St Dunstan's trainees learned craftwork of various kinds and in most cases became very skilful. They received much support through the St Dunstan's Sales Department, which supplied them with raw materials at cost price or cheaper. Finished goods were also bought by St Dunstan's and the craftsmen were paid whether or not the goods could be re-sold. The main objective was to maximise each man's earning power. Basket-makers, mat-makers and carpenters were encouraged to specialise in a small number of types of article for which there was a demand. By concentrating on relatively few designs, the carpenters especially were able to produce work more skilfully and quickly. Before commencing occupational training, the trainee was asked where he would be living and working. Then enquiries were made to learn what type of products were in demand locally and the trainee was informed which articles were most likely to be profitable.

Despite these efforts, sales were seriously affected during the economic slump of the early 1920s. Stocks of goods made by St Dunstaners mounted in the warehouse, although royal patronage had boosted the profile of the St Dunstan's shop in Regent Street. A subscription club launched with the aid of Bruce Bairnsfather's famous First World War cartoon character 'Old Bill' was a help and continued successfully into the 1930s. A Bairnsfather drawing on the membership certificates showed Old Bill helping a blinded soldier on the battlefield and turning to say, "Oi - give us an 'and mates - he can't see nothin'!" Members of the 'Old Bill Fraternity', among them the late Queen Mother (then the Duchess of York), undertook to pay small sums regularly into the club for the purchase of articles made by St Dunstaners.

There were already a few blind telephone operators in employment and telephonists were taught at the National Institute, and later at St Dunstan's. Most office switchboards at that time employed a drop shutter or doll's eye system to indicate lines or extensions calling, which a blind operator could detect. Pearson strongly believed that there was a good future for blind telephone operators: "There is a blind operator in the exchange at the National

Institute for the Blind and there are blind operators in the telephone exchanges of two metropolitan boroughs, both earning very good wages, both placed in open competition; and there are others elsewhere. In my opinion it is one of the departments of work for blind people which should and will be in future more developed". And so it has proved to be over the years and despite the development of new and much more sophisticated switchboards.

Not all Pearson's projects for opening up opportunities for blind workers were rewarded with such success. In 1916 he backed one particularly adventurous prospect: diving. Pearson described it as "an entirely new occupation for blind men and one for which I think they are particularly suited, as a diver in the ordinary way works in the dark. The usual work of a diver is harbour work...and the natural condition of the water in a harbour is generally such that it is impossible to see...It seems to me evident that a man who lives his life in the dark and is accustomed to always work in the dark will do so much better than a man who only does it for a few hours at a time".

The first St Dunstaner to train as a diver was then on his way to Dover to work for the Northern Salvage and Shipbreaking Co. of West Hartlepool, after receiving early diving training in a tank in London. Appropriately, 35-year-old Thomas Drummond had served with the Royal Naval Division (Engineers) and in civilian life he had been Second Engineer in a passenger liner. An Australian, Thomas had enlisted in New Zealand in October 1914 and was blinded at the Dardanelles in May 1915.

In April 1916 Drummond wrote to St Dunstan's: 'I have now been in the harbour three times in different depths of water, the greatest being 36 feet. The diving party, having finished their work on the *Halcyon* and removed to lodgings in Folkestone, I trust they will allow me to get some experience at the salvaging of this cargo'. Pearson shared his anxiety and wrote to Drummond's supervisor asking for practical work in the salvaging of the *Halcyon*: 'St Dunstan's will pay for his apprenticeship as so much depends on his progress, as regards establishing diving as an occupation for blind men'.

Later in the year Drummond was working in Hull and diving regularly, but there was a difficulty. Pearson had observed that a sighted diver needed an attendant on the surface to supervise ropes and air lines and concluded that, therefore, a blind diver would automatically have a sighted attendant and thus be at no disadvantage. The supervisor's reports from Hull indicated that Drummond needed four men at 2s 6d (25 pence) an hour! Although arrangements were made to make these payments, by the turn of the year Drummond was reporting plenty of promises but no work. He wished to return to St Dunstan's and the experiment was abandoned. Tom Drummond retrained as a masseur and finally went back to Australia, where he practised until he retired in 1935. He died in 1951. While this imaginative scheme had come to naught, many other St Dunstaners, trained in more mundane but lucrative occupations, were going home to their families and local communities. They were aided by settlement staff whose responsibility it was to find accommodation and work for those leaving.

Other St Dunstaners found that they were eventually able to return to their previous careers, and among them was Frederick Martin. In January 1918 Fred, a Scottish officer, came to Regent's Park. A Second Lieutenant in the 5th Gordon Highlanders, Fred had been serving for less than a year when his sight failed in 1915, while he was working as a musketry instructor. Before the war Fred had been a journalist on local newspapers, and with the instinct of a reporter he wrote many letters to his wife describing his new life. Some of them still survive and they give an insight into Pearson's methods of rehabilitation and the treatment of blinded officers at St Dunstan's.

An early letter describes the evening 'amusements' as he put it: 'Monday – dancing at the Queens Hall under the tuition of a professional with her lady pupils assisting. Tuesday – reading. Wed. – theatre. Thursday – guest night with some big pot to be the lion. Friday – Brighton for the weekend'.

He also sent her some 'Notes on Personalities'. They included:

'Clutha Mackenzie – Son of Sir Thomas of that ilk, the High Commissioner for New Zealand. He is about 20 and stands over six feet. Blinded in Gallipoli. Runs a paper for circulation among the troops of New Zealand now in France. He is very clever and unassuming and is one of the best known figures in colonial society. A great favourite and quite unspoiled.

'Ian Fraser – Also a blind young giant. He is from South Africa. Edits the St Dunstan's Review and is a darling in the eyes of Sir Arthur. Clever boy but spoilt. Engaged to...Miss Mace – otherwise Chips. Bright young lady. As secretary to Sir Arthur is a person of much importance. A good sort I think. There are many others but they are undistinguished except by their cheeriness and good fellowship.'

By February, Fred's training had begun in earnest and he wrote:

'At half past nine each morning I set out with two or three others and we walk from this place [21 Portland Place] to St Dunstan's. From ten to eleven I study Braille under the direction of Miss Edwards. From eleven to half past I type under the direction sometimes of one person and sometimes another. At half past eleven I proceed to netting and struggle with a hammock. A little after twelve we parade at what is known as the dug-out and pair off for the walk home.

'Twice a week we have instruction in the exercises of Muller [A type of physical drill using a wooden baton held in both hands]. This is timed for half past twelve and lasts for half an hour. In the afternoons if there is nothing better to do I return to St Dunstan's at two o'clock and there I net and practise typing. Something better to do consists of listening while somebody reads either a paper or a book. It may also mean a walk. Netting does not appeal to me. It is at the best only a means of killing time and to me, at all events, it is not a very pleasant means. There are also letters to be written and other things. For example this month I have written a short article for the St Dunstan's Review and I am under contract to do another. At the present stage of my knowledge it is impossible to study alone. Later on I hope to be able to devote more time to it.'

After six months of training, Fred resumed his career in journalism at the *Morning Post,* and later embarked on a political career. In 1922 Fred was returned as Liberal Member for East Aberdeenshire in the House of Commons, making him the first blind Member of the House since Henry Fawcett, who represented Brighton from 1865 to 1884 and became Postmaster General. While Frederick Martin's parliamentary career was cut short in 1924, when Robert Boothby defeated him, that same year Ian Fraser became MP for North St Pancras. Although he failed to regain his seat in three later elections, Martin was made CBE in 1942. He continued to play an important part in public life in Aberdeenshire as Vice-Convener of the County, and, not long before his death in 1950, he was appointed Convener.

But when Fred first arrived at St Dunstan's, his future was uncertain and on 16 January 1918 Arthur Pearson wrote to Fred's wife Flora to reassure her:

'*Dear Mrs Martin,*

I had a long talk with your husband yesterday evening. I am going at once to take up the question of his pension and hope that a satisfactory conclusion may be arrived at in this important matter. Your husband will also receive the very best advice in regard to his sight.

'*I feel sure that he will be happy and comfortable here and that you need be under no anxiety with regard to him. He is very keen on learning and will, I know, avail himself to the full of all the opportunities offered. He is taking his misfortune like a real man and is bound to come out all right.*

'*I hope that any time you would like to come to town for a visit you will do so. We shall always be glad to make comfortable arrangements for putting you up quite close by. I hope to have the pleasure of making your acquaintance before long.*'

It was through these small but thoughtful gestures that Pearson earned the confidence of his blinded soldiers. In a tribute on Sir Arthur's death, Fred Martin wrote, 'My task has been attempted in vain if I have not shown him to be one who commanded our admiration and our love'.

The many well-known visitors to the hostel and passers-by in the street who observed the activities there found their conceptions of the abilities of blind people totally changed. Long before the term was invented, a public relations exercise for the blind was in progress and Pearson's aim to establish his training centre in the heart of London was fully justified.

Chapter 3

St Dunstan's Versus Arsenal

*'We all come back slightly bruised, but walking an
inch taller because we had a go,'*
(Charles Daly, St Dunstaner, on skiing blind)

In the 1920s the casual stroller through Regent's Park might have seen one of the first experiments in sport and recreation for disabled people. Not only were preconceptions about the ability of blind people to take on remunerative occupations being overturned, but the sighted people of London could also watch blind men engaged in all kinds of sport.

Every week while training was in full swing in Regent's Park, around 200 St Dunstaners took part in the Saturday Sports. Programmes included the long-jump, skipping, rope climbing, shot put, relay races and – most popular of all – the 100 yards sprint. St Dunstan's annual report for 1920 proudly announced one 100-yard runner's time as 12.8 seconds, despite being guided by a rope and over rough ground. That record did not last long. The next annual report gave a list of records for the Saturday Sports:

'Running - 100 yards in 10.8 seconds
Walking - 3 miles in 29 minutes, 10 seconds
Walking - 100 yards in 17.6 seconds
Putting a 16lb Shot - 31 feet, 4 inches
Throwing the Cricket Ball - 82 yards
Throwing the Football - 31 yards
Three consecutive Standing Jumps - 27 feet, 9 inches
Climbing 30 ft rope - 10.6 seconds.'

The walking races were held around the Outer Circle of the park, while there were penalty shoot-outs against professional goalkeepers from famous London football clubs, and rowing on the lake. Two tug-of-war teams gave an exhibition match during the Royal Tournament at Olympia in July 1919 and were described in the press as follows, 'Clad in white ducks and sweaters, they marched into the arena in splendid style, with step as perfect as the sighted team of any regiment'.

Trainee masseur Tommy Milligan enjoyed these sports: "We used to get up at six in the morning, if we wished, have a cup of tea and go to the lake in Regent's Park and row. We were very keen on all kinds of things like that. Rowing was the only thing I was very good at really. It was very good exercise". Among the attractions may have been the sighted female coxswains:

"We had a lot of nice girls, some of them were shop girls. We were not very far from the West End, quite near Baker Street Station and they used to have their breakfasts early, get there about seven and take us out rowing, coxing our boats. Students from Bedford College for Women in Regent's Park also came. We were very serious about rowing. St Dunstan's formed a rowing club and we were trained by the President of the Vesta Rowing Club on the Thames. We had a racing four and we raced against schools like Worcester College for the Blind and the Emmanuel School, London, a famous rowing school".

As the years went on, St Dunstan's Annual Regattas were held at Putney. A St Dunstan's crew of four competed with guest entries, for instance a four from the House of Commons, and these events were widely reported in the national press. The St Dunstan's rowers made the headlines again, when a crew of four capsized and the cox, Sister Steine, made sure that her blind crew found the capsized boat and clung there until they were rescued.

The organisation and, not least, the St Dunstaners themselves accepted that there were risks for blind sportsmen despite measures to avoid them. After a time spent abroad, in 1926 Braille teacher Grace Stacey returned to help organise sports for St Dunstans in London. She recalled the spirit with which St Dunstaners responded to the challenges that she and Sports Officer Bill Tovell devised: "They were never nervous about anything. Never nervous or if they were, never showed it. They were keen on anything you suggested. I don't remember having anything turned down". Another innovation was goal-shooting. "Different clubs came. Arsenal was the special one. They used to train the men and they did it simply by calling out and they kicked. But you see we were so amateurish in those days – nobody knew anything – we were pioneers".

On 15 December 1920, the *Morning Post* published an account of a visit made by the Arsenal team to Regent's Park. Under the heading 'Williamson Tested' it read:

'Yesterday the final of the football competition was held for the Sir Arthur Pearson Challenge Cup. The Jazonians beat Hill's Athletic by five goals to four. Williamson, the well-known Arsenal goalkeeper was there to defend the goal against the attacks of the St Dunstan's men, and in addition the whole Arsenal team turned out to give a game to the sightless men. The Arsenal, although not at full strength, managed to win. They were blindfolded and scored four goals, but the St Dunstan's side could not beat Williamson. It was a great game.'

Did Ernie Williamson pull out a greater effort when St Dunstan's were shooting to save Arsenal from humiliating defeat by a blind team? We will never know. Williamson continued to visit Regent's Park to play football with St Dunstaners. A grateful Sir Arthur Pearson made a presentation of a rose bowl to the Arsenal and international keeper in recognition of all he did for the blinded sportsmen at Regent's Park.

With many St Dunstaners now settled all over the country in occupations and in their own homes, local clubs sprang up. Grace Stacey, who had taught Braille at Regent's Park, ran a London sports club and there were others in Brighton, Manchester and Birmingham, the latter organised by her old friend Avis Spurway. Avis became involved in St Dunstan's through her husband, a clergyman in the Royal Navy, and she maintained an absorbed interest in sport for blind people until her death in 1988. There was great rivalry between the clubs and they competed for a shield presented by Grace Stacey.

In later years Grace Stacey organised an annual Sports Day in Regent's Park and handicap walking races round the Outer Circle: "The Outer Circle was three miles and races were so many times round that. You had to have an escort but, of course, we VADs couldn't walk fast enough. I was rather short of training people so I rang up the local Guards Depot. After that I could have a man who was off duty any evening to help train and the Police always helped".

Grace Stacy and her colleagues soon found a new source of enthusiastic volunteers to help with sporting activities at St Dunstan's. Boy Scouts

17

became familiar young figures around Regent's Park. Paid a weekly wage of ten shillings, they acted as messengers and escorts for St Dunstaners in training. They all wore uniform and some of them went on to long careers as employees of St Dunstan's. George Zipfel became head of the Sales Department in later years, and Bert Cattermole served 50 years with the organisation.

Shortly before his retirement, Bert Cattermole recalled his early days at Regent's Park in an interview for the *St Dunstan's Review*. He started in 1926, aged 14, and was so small that St Dunstaners christened him 'Titch'. "We used to meet the men at the stations, take them to Victoria and put them on a train to Brighton", he explained. "Our official hours were 9-6, we used to bring in St Dunstaners who were training but lived out and, at the end of the working day see them home or on to buses and trains for their journeys".

The Scouts had a healthy respect for Matron Power, remembered Bert. "In those days the hospital matron was a real martinet. In many ways Matron Power was like this. She was boss of the VADs, the Sisters; boss over us boys – indirectly – and although she was very generous and a very warm-hearted woman, she was boss. All those single fellows she had there, she kept a motherly eye on them".

One Sports Day, Bert was sent to Paddington Station to meet two competitors:

"When I got there I found 22 of them! We couldn't get taxis in those days – St Dunstan's wasn't rich. It was tuppence on the bus and I hadn't got enough money for 22, so I sorted all the men out. Those with guiding sight I gave them a totally blind man each and we walked all up Praed Street and along Marylebone Road to the Green Man in Clarence Gate, where we were to have lunch.

"We Scouts used to help with the sports. It was a family affair; they used to come to London from all over the place. There would be a couple of hundred there on a Saturday afternoon. Then when the sports were all over we used to go to the grounds of St John's Lodge and have a slap-up tea. I remember all these things because of the slap-up teas! The first two years as a Boy Scout were really tip top."

At 16 the Boy Scouts usually left, but Bert was offered work in the Stationery Department and stayed on at St Dunstan's for another 48 years.

* * * * *

It was not long before the best St Dunstan's race walkers sought harder challenges by taking part in London to Brighton walks. There were many successes. Their participation in this event continued for over four decades. In that time, two St Dunstaners, Archie Brown and Les Dennis, became Centurions which, as the name implies, means they had completed 100 miles in less than 24 hours.

Over the following 40 years St Dunstaners also took to mountaineering in Snowdonia, challenged by a sighted and long term Welsh supporter of St Dunstan's, Bob Thomas. Bob, who was employed as a forester, walked and climbed in the mountains. When he asked, "Your St Dunstaners are very good race walkers on the flat, but how would they fare uphill?" his challenge was swiftly accepted. Escorted and guided by members of the Rhinog Mountain Rescue Team, groups climbed Snowdon, Cader Idris, Rhinog Fach and Tryfan with its famous twin vertical rocks on the summit, Adam and Eve. A team of four, Bill Shea, Ray Sheriff, Tom Lukes and Harry 'Johnnie' Cope scaled Tryfan despite its reputation as the only Welsh mountain that cannot be climbed without scrambling. Needless to say, none of them attempted the challenge to leap from the top of Adam on to Eve!

One of that team, Ray Sheriff, is believed to be the first blind man to scale the 2,800 foot ridge on the Horseshoe route to Crib Goch. Snow prevented Ray and his escorts from completing the Horseshoe to Snowdon, yet it was an outstanding achievement for a totally blind man and a tribute to his fitness in coping with a testing adventure. Perhaps his head for heights came from his experiences as a paratrooper during the war. Ray was blinded by a hand grenade in the Battle of Arnhem and for many years made an annual tandem parachute drop over Arnhem. On the thirty-fifth anniversary of the 'bridge too far' Ray was made a Freeman of Apeldoorn.

Another mountain sport enjoyed by St Dunstaners, which may well surprise the sighted reader, is skiing. For many years, Ray Hazan, blinded in Northern Ireland, led a group of war-blinded skiers on the slopes at one or other of the European winter resorts. There they teamed up with sighted guides, ski instructors or skilled army skiers These sighted guides skied either in front or behind their blind charge, calling commands to turn 'Left' or 'Right' or, in emergency, 'Sit Down!'

Charles Daly explained the attraction of skiing: "Starting down a ski slope blind is a bit hairy, relying on the directions of your sighted instructor. It brings excitement into what really is a dull old life and excitement is a form of release. We all come back slightly bruised but walking an inch taller because we had a go". Ray Hazan put it more poetically, "What makes the holiday so exciting is that first moment on the snow. When you hear, ringing in your ear, the commands to turn from your guide, to feel the wind in your hair, the swish of the snow against your skis in the turn and the hiss as you ski straight. It is to breathe in the clean air, to sense the vistas of mountain tops, snow covered fir trees and the stillness that nature can create".

Sir Arthur Pearson was right: the blind *can* perceive without seeing! The First World War pioneer St Dunstaners were newly blind men who, through determination and fitness, were proving themselves worthy competitors with sighted athletes in sport, as well as being capable of success in many kinds of employment. What was happening in St Dunstan's surprised the post-war world. Pearson, the man who gave these young men the inspiration and the opportunity to make these achievements was greatly praised and admired. In 1916 he was made a baronet and in 1917 he became Knight Grand Cross of the Order of the British Empire.

Even in the formal atmosphere of a Government Departmental Committee on the Welfare of the Blind in 1916, the Chairman, the Rt Hon W. Hayes Fisher, MP, was moved to praise Pearson: "I cannot allow you to leave the chair with only the ordinary customary expression of thanks. I could not help thinking of you the other day, when reading the words *lux e tenebris*; out of your darkness light has come, and will for many a person who is similarly afflicted to yourself".

Chapter 4

After-care and Independence

'One of the greatest movements that has ever been started for the amelioration of the condition of the blind,'
(Arthur Pearson, 1916)

P earson's vision of establishing blind people as active members of the community was not confined to the ex-servicemen of St Dunstan's. His arrival in the blind world as a man with a mission was a case of the right person catching the right moment in history. A shift in attitudes towards blind people was under way before the turn of the century. Prior to this the use of terms like 'Asylum for the Blind' and 'Society for the Relief of the Indigent Blind' were signs of a negative approach to the handicap. In the late 1700s there was even a charity founded in York for, amongst other things, the 'blind, nearly blind and idiotic'. We must hope that the last was not meant to apply to the blind people!

However, times were changing. In the 1800s, as well as schools and homes for the blind, sheltered workshops were set up where blind workers would be employed to produce articles for sale. Blind soldiers may have been included in these projects, as it would seem that they were regarded as no different to civilian blind people before the coming of St Dunstan's.

Prospects of more general employment for the blind were also being explored. Between 1883 and 1914 a series of national and international conferences on the welfare, education and employment of blind people were held in Britain. The London Institute of Massage for the Blind was founded in 1900 and became the National Institute of Massage for the Blind in 1908. In 1914, the year Pearson was elected as President of the National Institute for the Blind, the Local Government Board appointed a departmental committee to 'Consider the present position of the blind in the United Kingdom, and the means available for (a) their industrial or professional training, and (b) their assistance; and to make recommendations'.

By 1916 at the St Dunstan's Headquarters in Regent's Park there was a practical and successful demonstration of the means that the 1914 committee were looking for. Pearson's energy and innovative approach to new fields of employment for blind people led to an invitation to be a member of the 1916 departmental committee. He also gave evidence on the setting up of St Dunstan's, its finances and training programmes. Responding to questions about the future Pearson's answers reveal a vision much wider than the welfare of St Dunstaners. This was perhaps not surprising, as Pearson, to use a newly coined term, was himself a 'civilian blind person'.

Asked about the future, Pearson told the committee that he believed that St Dunstan's, "as it exists now", would cease its operations presumably within a year of the end of hostilities. His priority, he explained, was to train St Dunstaners and get them back into work, but then continue to support them. "There is no real object in training these men and setting them up and sending them out into the world to look after themselves if they are not to be looked after adequately and properly in the future. They must be provided with their raw material, they must be helped with regard to the marketing of their goods...or helped to secure continuity of employment if they are engaged in some occupation which does not involve the actual making of goods".

Pearson confirmed that the National Institute for the Blind (NIB) had also started a department for this purpose and hoped to extend it to blind home-workers throughout the UK. "I think it is likely to prove one of the greatest movements that has ever been started for the amelioration of the condition of the blind. The blinded soldier has afforded the opportunity of making an experiment which it would have been very difficult, if not impossible, to make otherwise".

Pearson thought that both civilian blind people and blinded soldiers would be best served by the creation of a general after-care scheme. During this period Pearson, as President of the NIB, was urging the centralisation of work for the blind. He made efforts to take over the National Massage Institution and finally came to an agreement with its council, with the proviso that the Massage Institution's name would be preserved and 'that the work of training the blind people will be conducted under medical supervision'.

Pearson had also engaged a suitable massage instructor for St Dunstan's at a salary of £200 per annum and reported that work would be commenced forthwith in rooms set apart in the institute for the purpose. By 1916 Pearson had also set up the Home Teaching Branch of 24 home teachers, with the aid of the Home Teaching Society and steps were being made to link their work with after-care.

His most ambitious plan was the unification of fundraising for blindness charities over the whole country. A standing committee was formed and negotiations including the Ministry of Health and the many local societies continued for several years until a meeting of all concerned in London in April 1920. The discussion was largely antagonistic to Pearson's proposals. There were no resolutions, no policy, and it was obvious that the time was not opportune.

Just over a month later Pearson wrote a letter to *The Times* criticising the recently passed Bill to Promote the Welfare of Blind Persons:

'We wish that the Bill were wider in its scope and that there could be added to it a clause by which local institutions could be provided with funds sufficient to enable them to carry out adequately a system of caring for those living in their neighbourhood, but not working in their premises...workshop[s] throughout the country should be placed in a position to care for the scattered blind in the neighbourhood of which it is the centre, training them for home work, supplying...raw material, and assisting them to market their goods.'

He revealed that the success of the adoption of this method at St Dunstan's showed that 'tremendous advantage can be extended to blind civilians'. He continued: 'Some three years ago the National Institute for the Blind...started a widespread organisation of the kind for blind civilians but at the end of last year it became evident that [it was]...beyond the resources of any individual institution'.

Pearson was now seeking government finance, his efforts to mobilise the fundraising potential of the majority of the country's blind organisations having failed. Although his rise in the blind world had been meteoric he was still a comparative newcomer and, perhaps, he had been over-optimistic. The signs had been there very soon after the establishment of the Blinded Soldiers and Sailors Hostel. On 15 May 1915 an advertisement appeared in *The Times* that greatly perturbed the Care Committee. It was nothing less than an appeal from the London Association for the Blind competing directly with the work of the St Dunstan's Care Committee. Wordy and somewhat overwritten, it included this passage:

'In due course of time the blinded soldier is discharged from hospital. All that is possible has been done but in vain. The sentence of eternal darkness has been passed. He is blind for life. Of course, the War Office gives him a pension but that will not teach him 'how to be blind', how to go about, how to learn a new trade and how to support himself in comfort so as to be financially independent of others.

'Provision for these needs is being made by the London Association for the Blind, who have secured an ideally placed house at Worthing for the reception of blinded soldiers and sailors both British and Belgian and, where there are no soldiers and sailors, of other blind people.'

The advertisement was signed by Dr G.H. Rosedale DD, Honorary Secretary of the London Association.

It must have been particularly galling to Pearson, the arch publicist, to be so soon challenged and by someone echoing his own words. Dr Rosedale could have hardly been unaware of the advanced stage the NIB's plans had reached, as there had already been press publicity. Sir Washington Ranger undertook to meet Dr Rosedale to explain the situation created by his advertisement. However, the Reverend Doctor would not change his attitude.

The War Office was called in and issued an official communication on 25 May. To be doubly sure, the Blinded Soldiers and Sailors Care Committee placed a two-column advertisement in *The Times* of 29 May. Under a large heading, 'THE BLINDED SOLDIER', readers of *The Times* learned that:

'The Secretary of State for War has approved the arrangements which have been made for providing additional accommodation at the Blinded Soldiers' Hostel, at St Dunstan's, Regent's Park to an extent which will enable 120 men to be cared for and trained there. These arrangements include the erection of spacious workshops, besides those already in use, and considerable additions of a temporary character to the house. It is officially announced that the War Office approves the work of the Blinded Soldiers Care Committee, and is satisfied that this organisation will meet the needs of all those who may be blinded during the war.'

The big guns of the War Office were too much for the London Association and the Care Committee received a letter from Sir Frederick Milner, stating that 'Dr Rosedale's belligerent attitude would cease'. What must have meant more to the committee was the Secretary of State's unqualified approval of their work.

* * * * *

The confidence of the War Office was not misplaced, as proven by the steady stream of blinded soldiers leaving Regent's Park and confidently entering upon their trades and professions in the community. The first massage students, including Private Thomas Milligan, had passed out. Their marks ranged from 56 to 68 per cent and all were placed in employment. However, more new St Dunstaners were arriving and even the additional accommodation mentioned in press reports would soon prove to be inadequate.

Around St Dunstan's Villa other properties were brought into use as annexes. A house in Sussex Place, just a few minutes walk away, was rented for the use of the men learning massage. Equally close was Townsend House, providing room for 20 St Dunstaners. Just beyond Sussex Place, three large houses in Cornwall Terrace were also acquired and connected to accommodate another 100 men. Further afield, a convalescent annexe of two adjoining houses at Blackheath, was placed at St Dunstan's disposal by the NIB. In 1917 the NIB also offered West House, in Kemp Town, Brighton for the use of St Dunstan's as a holiday home and convalescent centre. In 1918 the Federation of Grocers' Associations of the United Kingdom donated £11,000 to cover the cost of purchase and subsequent equipping of the building for its new role.

The main reason for the influx of new blinded casualties was the costly and terrible series of attacks on German lines in the summer of 1916, which became known as the Battle of the Somme. Among the newly blinded men brought home from the battlefield to St Mark's Hospital in London, was 18-year-old Lieutenant Ian Fraser. Arthur Pearson was away, so Fraser's first visitor was Pearson's assistant Irene Mace, who brought him the customary Braille watch. She also read him a letter from Pearson.

In his book, *My Story of St Dunstan's*, Fraser wrote of the great encouragement he derived from the Braille watch and the letter, showing just how effective the gift of the watch could be:

'It was an ordinary watch without a glass and with little raised dots round the outside edge. There was a dot against each numeral, with double dots at the quarters. The hands were slightly raised and a little flatter and stronger than ordinary watch hands. A hunter lid shut down and protected the face. I held the watch in my hand and felt the face with my thumb. For the first time since I was wounded I was able to tell the time...It was an extraordinary pleasure to find that it was just as easy to do with the hands as with the eyes. Perhaps there were other things.'

The letter Fraser received was, of course, Pearson's routine one, but it survives, and gives an insight into Pearson's methods. He wrote:

'Dear Lieutenant Fraser,

I had a letter this morning from Captain Ormond telling me of the bad luck that has befallen you and I am writing to tell you how very truly and sincerely I sympathise with you and how sorry I am that I am prevented from coming to see you at present...I am afraid that at the moment the future must look very black to you but I assure you from my own experience – for I am quite blind and lost my sight while strong and vigorous in every other respect – that blindness does not involve the dreary and empty life which at first it seems to necessitate. In a little while you will find yourself as I do happy, occupied and with any amount of interest in your life...

'An undue proportion of very young officers have lost their sight at the front but all of them I am glad to say have found their lives as blind men immeasurably more happy than seems at first possible. I hope that a little later on you will like to join the other officers whose sight has been badly damaged, and learn the various things which will be useful to you in your new mode of life. I can promise you a great deal of interest and enjoyment in doing this and I know that you will be happy as a member of the family party at Portland Place.'

So Ian Fraser joined the family party. His future would be inextricably linked with St Dunstan's. His own training completed, Fraser was put in charge of the new after-care department and in 1918 he married Irene Mace, his first visitor from St Dunstan's.

That same year there were over 600 men at Regent's Park and in the annexes. In the spring they received a surprise visit from Queen Mary, who had made up her mind that she should go and see casualties from the latest fighting. She learned that few patients had yet reached the London hospitals and had 'felt this was really useless', so 'visited St Dunstan's instead'.

More than 400 St Dunstaners had completed their training by this time, and many of them wrote to Regent's Park reporting on their progress. Some were able to return to their former professions. Lieutenant Geoffrey Pemberton, a Tank Commander with the Queen's Royal West Surrey Regiment, was blinded in 1918 at the Battle of the Somme. After retraining at St Dunstan's, at Arthur Pearson's suggestion he decided to return to his career in accountancy, although at the time there was no precedent of a blind accountant:

'When I went to St Dunstan's it never occurred to me that I might go back to my old business as a chartered accountant. But with you I saw that many had taken up their former work with extraordinary success. Encouraged by this and by your optimism I determined to try myself. I have been back at work now for six months, but though that is a very short time, I think there is no doubt that all is well...All my old clients say they are absolutely satisfied; they are business men and I don't think over sentimental.'

Mat maker, Patrick F.C. Fleetwood, (formerly a Private in the 1st Worcester Regiment and wounded at the Dardanelles in 1915) wrote:

'My wife has gone to the market today with mats and netted articles; I hope she will sell out. I wonder how many of our fellows have a shot at getting their own dinner. Today I am looking after a big fire, several pots and pans, doing a bit of baking, giving the dog his dinner and doing a bit of matting into the bargain, and I am enjoying it. I do not omit to lay the cloth properly because I am alone. I can wash the dishes, too.'

Poultry farmer, Second Lieutenant Stephens reported:

'I have been very busy clearing the land around about the place of bracken. I cleared about three acres myself with a sickle and did not

find loss of sight much of a handicap in doing so. I also cut down a
few trees of about eight inches in diameter without chopping off any
toes. Our fowls are laying well, which is very gratifying, as none of
our neighbours' hens are laying.'

Andrew Nugee was able to report success in his studies at Oxford University where, despite time lost through an operation, he had received his Bachelor of Arts degree: 'My next move is to Bishop's Hostel at Lincoln, where I am going to read for Holy Orders at the Theological College...after which I hope to be ordained'. Nugee duly became a minister of the Church of England in 1921.

Andrew Nugee's success opened the way for five other St Dunstaners to enter Holy Orders over the years, despite the negative attitude shown by Church leaders when Pearson raised the subject in 1916. The Bishop of Oxford responded that 'he would have supposed it was out of the question to ordain a blind man to Holy Orders unless he had exceptional gifts as a preacher', while the Archbishop of York felt that bishops 'would decline to ordain blind men for very obvious reasons unless the candidate had 'special qualifications...remarkable in their character'.

In contrast the Archbishop of Canterbury expressed his support for St Dunstaners hoping to enter the Church: 'I have always felt that blindness ought to not be considered as an absolutely fatal barrier to ordination'. A candidate would require 'remarkable personal gifts' and eloquence, he admitted, as well as 'power as theological student and thinker'. At the same time, he also felt that 'a man who possesses no more than the ordinary qualifications of an ordination candidate would, I fear, be at so grave a disadvantage if he were blind that I could not encourage him to seek Holy Orders'. Andrew Nugee must have done rather well.

Another man passing out was George Killingbeck and Pearson's farewell letter to him reveals the support offered to all St Dunstaners leaving the training centre. Dated 6 April 1920 it began: 'I am very sorry your time at St Dunstan's has come to an end, and I hope that you will look back upon your stay here with pleasure, and that it will prove to have been of lasting benefit to you. You are one of the fellows whom it has been a real pleasure to have with us'. The letter confirmed the gift of Braille machine and typewriter earned by Killingbeck's success in proficiency tests and that he would have free life membership of the National Library for the Blind, ('I do hope you will keep up your reading').

Pearson concluded the letter:

'Although I regret that owing to the loss of your left arm you have been unable to take up any of the occupations taught here, I am glad that you have made good use of your opportunity to have elocution and speech lessons, to enable you to take up the position as a member of the Campaigning Staff of the National Institute for the Blind...My good wishes go with you for your success in this work.'

After he left Regent's Park Killingbeck's sight recovered sufficiently, as he reported to St Dunstan's, to enable him to ride a motorcycle. For seven years he worked in insurance, but his sight failed once more and he was re-admitted to St Dunstan's in 1929. This time he worked for St Dunstan's Appeals Department, until 1940 when he became a Braille instructor. Killingbeck taught the new generation of St Dunstaners until 1967 – the last few years in a voluntary capacity – for a record 37 years service.

Chapter 5

Appeals and Arguments

'They gave their sight – what will you give?'
(St Dunstan's First World War appeals slogan)

T he large numbers of young blinded men returning from the war in France had a dramatic effect on the public. Local sympathy was particularly strongly aroused by the return of a blinded soldier to his home town. In 1918 Billy Clough went back to Ramsbottom, Lancashire, after being blinded while serving with the Lancashire Fusiliers. His niece recalled a poem circulated in the town to raise money for St Dunstan's. Part of it read:

'On every front throughout the war some lads from Rams have been,
In Egypt and Salonika, France and Russia, fighting they have seen,
And when the war is over what are we going to do,
To help these gallant lads of ours who've helped to pull us through?
Some will be crippled many ways; one we know is blind,
We must try to help poor Billy Clough and also bear in mind,
The Government may provide an arm or leg and make it work alright,
But it is beyond the power of human aid to give a blind man sight.'

Appeals by the National Institute for the Blind on behalf of the Blinded Soldiers and Sailors Care Committee exploited this public feeling, using the work of artists who depicted poignant scenes. For example, a series of picture postcards included a blinded soldier on the battlefield, hands covering his eyes, stumbling towards an open trench. Another drawing showed a young man in a deckchair, one hand stroking his dog, while above his head floated memories of the sporting activities he could no longer pursue. Slogans like 'Blinded for you' and 'They gave their sight – what will you give?' strengthened the public's feelings of indebtedness towards these blinded soldiers. Until the coming of the guide dog these were probably the most powerful images in fundraising for blind organisations.

Their resonance was illustrated by the St Dunstan's Treasurer, Ernest Kessell's report to the Blinded Soldiers and Sailors Care Committee in January 1916. Over the previous Christmas period subscriptions had amounted to no less than £9,000 (around £350,000 today). However, one individual, Kenneth Bilbrough, the head of a shipping company, collected £6,000 only a month later. Another measure of the appeal of blinded soldiers is that in March 1916, for fear of competition, the Red Cross and St John offered £20,000 for the withdrawal of a flag day for St Dunstan's.

A few St Dunstaners, like George Killingbeck, became personal representatives for the charity, giving talks and encouraging fundraising efforts. Their success brought dissent with other charities, however, and one of the first of these difficulties was with the newly formed Scottish National Institution for the War Blinded. In 1915 a hostel for Scottish blinded soldiers was established at Newington House in Edinburgh, under the auspices of the Royal Blind Asylum and School. Early in 1916 a stirring of Scottish national sentiment led to a number of speeches and correspondence in the Scottish press and this brought a reaction from St Dunstan's. In the altercation that followed it became clear that part of the problem lay in fundraising.

On 9 March 1916 the *Edinburgh Evening Despatch* published a suspiciously articulate letter from a St Dunstaner, Private Duncan Matheson McLean, a regular soldier from the 11th Royal Scots, who had only just commenced training in Regent's Park. Under the heading 'Home for Blind Soldiers – A Scottish Soldier's Testimony', he wrote: 'As a Scottish patient from St Dunstan's at present on holiday in Edinburgh, perhaps I may be allowed to express an opinion on the controversy raised by those interested in the establishment of a training hostel in this city. The impression one would gather from the speeches made and the correspondence on the subject is that the Scottish blinded soldiers are pining to come to Edinburgh'.

As a Glaswegian, McLean pointed out with some feeling that not all Scottish soldiers were Edinburgh men and that those from Glasgow or Dundee would be as much at home in Regent's Park as in Edinburgh. He continued:

'Those of us who know the limited capacities of Newington mansion houses as compared with St Dunstan's realise how badly handicapped the promoters of the Edinburgh scheme will be in their endeavours to provide the means of instruction that St Dunstan's patients have become accustomed to...We Scottish soldiers in St Dunstan's cannot forget that Mr C.A. Pearson ferreted us out of various hospitals throughout the country and immediately interested himself in our welfare before the Edinburgh critics ever gave a thought to the existence of blind soldiers. Now that St Dunstan's has justified its existence surely it would be better to support it rather than set up what must be, for some time at least, an experimental institution.'

A Scottish soldier training in Regent's Park would not necessarily lose touch with his friends in Scotland or became an expatriate, he commented. 'Some of us will be glad to get back to Scotland among our friends there but meanwhile does it really matter whether our training is obtained in Edinburgh or London as long as we obtain the training that will fit us to fight the battle of life'. As it happened, when he completed his training, Duncan McLean became a poultry farmer near Reading in Berkshire, though many others returned to the country of their birth.

Some of them may have been among the 11 St Dunstaners who signed a second letter, published in the *Scotsman* on 15 March, endorsing all that Duncan McLean had written. They wrote: 'It is very kind of the authorities of the Edinburgh Blind Asylum to offer us the use of their establishment but we do not wish to enter that or any other institution for the blind. We believe that St Dunstan's – which is not in the ordinary sense an institution for the blind but a special place, specially designed for our needs and happiness – is in every way a better place for us'. Then came a paragraph which was to be seized upon by Dr Thomas Burns, Chairman of Directors of the Royal Asylum: 'We think that if our friends in Scotland wish to show their interest in us they cannot do this in a better way than by sending contributions to the funds of St Dunstan's where we are so happy and well cared for'.

Dr Burns had no doubt as to the authorship of the letters when he responded in a letter to the *Scotsman* on 16 March:

'To prevent any misunderstanding it is only fair that I should be permitted to say, in reply to letters sent to the press by Mr Pearson

and signed by blinded soldiers that the directors have no desire to take away from St Dunstan's any Scotsman who fares so sumptuously there...We want Scottish blinded soldiers and sailors to come to us direct from the hospital for the training necessary to enable them to work for themselves. We have no desire by luxurious living to spoil their future usefulness.

'It would seem from the last paragraph in the signed letter that with London it is a matter of Scottish subscriptions. With us our interest in our Scottish blinded soldiers is a matter of national sentiment and national independence...People in Scotland have to remember that the London National Institute for the Blind, which claims in its circulated leaflets that it has undertaken the care of the blinded soldiers at St Dunstan's as a branch of its work, is a trading concern in direct rivalry with our Edinburgh Institution. It would be well to know how much of the money subscribed in Scotland goes to Scottish blinded soldiers and how much into the general funds of the London National Institute for the Blind.'

This strong stuff provoked Pearson to reply in the *Scotsman* on 18 March. Answering Dr Burns's question on how much money was diverted to the NIB he wrote: 'in one word, 'none'. All money subscribed in Scotland, or elsewhere, is devoted to their use and to no other purpose'. But the Scots were not to be moved. The affair dragged on, and the Ministry of Pensions became involved after Pearson complained of the 'inadequacy' of arrangements for after-care at Newington House. After reports on both establishments by Sir Edward Stewart an agreement was finally reached in 1919 through the Ministry, which enabled existing St Dunstaners to choose for themselves between Newington House and St Dunstan's with a similar choice for new trainees; a situation that still exists today. There was also a shared appeal for a period before St Dunstan's agreed not to raise funds north of the border.

While this dispute dragged on, St Dunstan's was doing extremely well at fundraising, especially in trying out new methods. In July 1915, Percy White wrote to the St Dunstan's Care Committee with a novel suggestion to set up a National Carol League, 'formed of persons of at least fair voices...in each town and village throughout the country'. A 'well-known person' in the district would direct each branch and as Christmas approached groups of two or three members wearing badges or armlets would call at houses singing carols. A postscript in the margin read: 'Selecting the biggest and better class houses first and working downwards'. The Carol League was quickly off the ground and carol singing over Christmas in 1915 raised £6,000. Throughout the 1930s the Carol League flourished, and its members proudly wore a specially designed enamel badge.

A group of blind employees of the National Institute for the Blind also began, late in 1915, to give concerts organised by Lady Pearson, which made more than £4,000 in a year – a considerable sum of money at that time. In 1917, Lady Pearson wrote to the NIB Council, 'I am not content with the result of £7,945 for the year and I most sincerely hope to double that amount'. From all this it can be seen that charitable appeals were capable of raising big money. Pearson's idealistic aim for a national appeals agreement among charities for the blind had always been doomed to failure. In the future there would never be a realistic chance of success.

*   *   *   *   *

In 1916 Sir Arthur Pearson had confidently forecast the establishment of a nation-wide after-care service in contact with local workshops or home-workers, to cater for all blind people. This developed the plans he had formed in the very earliest days of the Blinded Soldiers and Sailors Care Committee and looked ahead to the National Institute for the Blind 'taking over the after-care of the soldiers and sailors...when St Dunstan's is closed'. In March 1920 the NIB set up an Estate Department to rent houses, shops, and poultry farms for St Dunstan's men.

Yet within just six months the picture had changed and the first steps were being taken towards the total separation of St Dunstan's from the National Institute. What made Pearson change his mind and the direction of his policies so radically? At that time the NIB was beginning to live somewhat beyond its means and Pearson of all people would have been aware of this. He may have decided to save his brainchild St Dunstan's from suffering financially through affiliation with the NIB. The Ministry of Health had also withdrawn from any involvement in the national after-care scheme. Pearson's request for greater government help had gone unheeded.

In October 1920 a report by a government committee was submitted to the NIB asking whether it was time for the responsibility for after-care to pass from them to St Dunstan's. The report caused a stir among the NIB's members, as it suggested that the NIB should be responsible for the upkeep of St Dunstan's hostels, then in Brighton, St Leonards-on-Sea, Cheltenham, Blackheath and Ilkley. This would enable the NIB to continue appealing for blinded soldiers, justifying the NIB letterhead, which bore the words: 'To which is affiliated St Dunstan's Blinded Soldiers and Sailors After-Care Fund'. The NIB would continue to manage properties and funds belonging to the Blinded Soldiers After-Care Committee and that the affiliation of St Dunstan's to the NIB would continue. The process of separation had begun.

The next step came on 6 February 1921 when the NIB received a further report from the committee 'elucidated by Sir Arthur Pearson'. As a result the NIB Executive Committee passed a number of resolutions. They decreed that the administration of St Dunstan's and the NIB should be kept distinct; that all properties and investments of St Dunstan's would be transferred to that organisation, as should the NIB Estate Department; that the NIB and its branches should cease to appeal for St Dunstan's although appeals work should be co-ordinated and finally that the Blind Musicians Concert Party and the Carol League should be conducted for the benefit of both organisations.

The separation was complete and the last resolutions on appeals would turn into thorny questions in the future. In the weeks that followed, the affairs of the two organisations were untangled. Meanwhile the financial situation of both charities was deteriorating. The NIB was forced into drastic economies, while St Dunstan's was selling £100,000 of war bonds to meet expenditure.

Chapter 6

'The Stayer's Handicap'

'The Remington Typewriter Co.'s mechanic [has] devised a
most novel machine, which enables Sergeant Nichols, who,
besides being blind, has lost both his hands, to typewrite.'
(*St Dunstan's Review*, 1917)

One aspect of the work carried out at St Dunstan's hardly figured in the publications issued by the organisation. It was hinted at only by a brief entry in the annual report of 1918, under the heading 'Sincere thanks are offered to,' above a long list of surgeons and physicians, including ophthalmologists, ear, nose and throat specialists, nerve specialists and dentists. Heading the list were two ophthalmic surgeons: Major Arthur Ormond and Mr (later Sir) Arnold Lawson. Major Ormond was responsible for blinded servicemen at the 2nd London General Hospital at St Mark's, while Arnold Lawson looked after those entering St Dunstan's by different routes.

In 1922 Lawson wrote an account of his work, *War Blindness at St Dunstan's,* and paid tribute to the ready assistance always available from London-based doctors and surgeons in treating health problems facing St Dunstaners other than blindness. He wrote: 'The vast majority of the wounded were suffering from some chronic trouble not severe enough' to warrant hospital treatment, but still requiring daily care. 'Consequently, a large dispensary, staffed by a Sister, with a fully trained nurse and several VADs, was one of the earliest necessities of St Dunstan's'. Later a second large dispensary was added together with another smaller one. Each of the two main dispensaries had adjoining fully-equipped consulting rooms. Two doctors made daily visits for general health care. They were Dr E. Chittenden Bridges and Dr Arthur F. Gervis.

Eventually a small private hospital was established close to St Dunstan's in Sussex Place. It could accommodate 27 patients and many operations on St Dunstaners were performed there. Arnold Lawson was able to conclude that: 'Nearly all the men left St Dunstan's in far better health than when they arrived, and, as regards their eyes, quite a number of cases proved amenable in some degree to treatment, with or without operative measures, as the case might be; so that they were able to leave the Hostel with their little sight made stable, and often distinctly improved. In a few cases, alas! a very few, the improvement was so great that it became no longer necessary for them to be treated and trained as blind men'.

Arnold Lawson's statement brings home the fact that, contrary to the opinion held by most of the sighted public, blindness did not and does not imply total darkness. In recent times the World Health Organisation suggests registration as blind if a person cannot see two fingers raised at face level more than ten feet away. St Dunstan's definition of blindness, accepted by the government department dealing with pensions, was that a soldier was recognised as blind if he was, 'unable to read or write or to do ordinary work in an ordinary way'.

The ophthalmic surgeons had the task of assessing eligibility for entry to St Dunstan's and Arnold Lawson described some men as 'borderland', with slightly too much sight for admission. One of the reasons for their refusal was that, 'They formed a group of men who still retained a little useful and very precious sight, barely sufficient for earning any sort of living and maintained so precariously that it would be endangered by the learning of handicrafts such as those taught to the blinded men'. This opinion might well be challenged today and certainly in recent times such borderline cases have been offered preliminary training. Records are kept so that these individuals can be recalled for more tests to detect further deterioration in their sight, which might qualify them for admission.

In this quite literally 'grey area' there is always the possibility of fraud or malingering, as Arnold Lawson put it:

'Some of these cases were very tiresome and puzzling, because the applicants were much too artful to claim complete blindness, which they knew would soon become an impossible role, as well as a condition easily detected. Many cases of blindness at St Dunstan's were the result of injury to the visual cortex, and showed nothing by examination of the eyes themselves, so that a story of this kind had to be treated with caution. My usual plan in such cases was to

assume that the man was what he said himself to be and I admitted him to the Hostel with particular directions that he should be watched.

'For a few days all would go well, and then, after a little while, the man would almost always become careless and at times forget his part. For instance he would be noticed walking to a chair and placing it in a convenient place for seeing an entertainment, or altering the time of his watch, or give himself away in some other simple manner. But at one period of the War we were so bothered with these malingerers that we got a detective into the hostel, who pretended to be a blind man. He played his part extremely well and proved a great success, speedily unearthing one or two cases about which we were doubtful.'

Arnold Lawson was able to quote a total figure of 1,833 servicemen blind as a result of the First World War just 18 months after its end. He made a distinction between wound-blindness and disease-blindness pointing out that 26 per cent of admissions were due to the latter. However, he forecast more admissions from sight deteriorating as a consequence of disease in future years and, after both world wars, this was borne out to a much greater extent than he could have foreseen.

In *War Blindness at St Dunstan's* Arnold Lawson also gives a series of detailed descriptions of the more medically interesting individual cases that he dealt with. Many had serious additional injuries, like damaged hands. St Dunstan's was, of course, seized with the importance of hands and fingers to a blind man. Those who came with injuries to their hands received special treatment from skilled masseurs, advised by eminent specialists.

One of these men was Nathaniel Downs, known as 'Drummer', his rank in the 1st Loyal North Lancashire Regiment. Drummer's wounds were extensive and involved the amputation of his right arm and loss of four fingers of his left hand. Fortunately he had some guiding vision remaining. Supplied with artificial hands, which were at that time for appearances only, and special appliances and gloves, he learned to use a typewriter. He made good use of what grip function remained in his left hand to hold a drumstick to play the bass drum in the St Dunstan's Rag Time Band, with the top half of a cymbal attached to his right arm. In 1923 Drummer Downs joined St Dunstan's appeal staff and worked for the charity until after the Second World War.

Only two St Dunstaners survived the First World War with the loss of both hands. One was Charles Kelk, who in fact entered St Dunstan's in 1952, his sight having deteriorated many years after his wounding. The other was Sergeant Alan Nichols, who was admitted in 1917. Nichols's double disability was a spur to the ingenuity of St Dunstan's staff. Attempting to find answers to such serious problems for individuals became a regular part of the services they offered to war-blinded men and women and, after the Second World War, led to the formation of a fully-fledged Research Department.

Nichols was a regular soldier serving with the Durham Light Infantry and was among Kitchener's Expeditionary Force, which went to France in 1914. He was wounded that year and returned to this country, where he became a Bombing Instructor. In 1916 while setting a practice charge there was a premature explosion. Nichols's assistant was killed, but he survived to become St Dunstan's first blind and handless casualty.

In May 1917 Sergeant Nichols was fit enough to join his colleagues in Regent's Park. Two years later he passed his typewriting test! Typing test? Yes, and an article in *St Dunstan's Review* explained how it was done:

'Miss Knutford, who has devoted so much of her time and skill to the care and treatment of St Dunstaners who have lost their arms and hands or had them badly damaged, together with our own and the Remington Typewriter Co.'s mechanic have devised a most novel machine, which enables Sergeant Nichols, who, besides being blind, has lost both his hands, to typewrite.

'The machine is an ordinary No.7 Remington Typewriter. A lever has been fixed to the shift key in such a manner as to make it possible to change from capitals to ordinary type by an arrangement of the knee, while at the back of the machine are fitted supports which carry a roll of paper, and this makes it possible for Nichols to type a large number of letters without having to get someone to put in a new sheet of paper every few minutes. The keyboard and space bar are covered by a detachable metal case, with a funnel-shaped hole immediately over each key, and steps to indicate each row of keys. Nichols has an attachment fitted to his artificial hand in the shape of a round peg with which he strikes the key.'

After completing his training, Alan Nichols tried to establish himself in business. His first venture, a greengrocer and florist business initially flourished to the point where he opened a second shop, but in 1922 he sold it. A brief essay into hairdressing and a beauty parlour ended in a loss. He finally found his niche as a speaker and fundraiser for St Dunstan's, and continued with this work for 34 years. Using attachments to his artificial limbs to enable him to use tools, Alan Nichols found gardening a rewarding hobby. When the Second World War began he built his own air raid shelter. Nichols would become the model for the many more handless casualties in the Second World War and in 1943, when St Dunstan's Research and Development Department was formed, the new head, Peter Nye, spent some time with Alan Nichols, studying his problems and his means of overcoming them.

Alan Nichols was one of the characters of St Dunstan's. Kitchener's Expeditionary Force, in which he had served, was described by the Kaiser as, "Britain's contemptible little army". With the wry humour of the British soldier Alan Nichols and his colleagues who wore the 1914 or Mons Star called themselves the 'Old Contemptibles'. He founded the St Dunstan's branch of the Old Contemptibles and, with a slightly macabre sense of humour, he instituted the 'Stayer's Handicap' to give his comrades, as he put it, the will to live. There was a silver cup and a 'purse' of £100 in National Savings Certificates for the last surviving St Dunstan's Old Contemptible.

The competition was established in April 1955, but Nichols soon realised that the oldest members of the 51 starters had "about a snowball in hell's chance against some of the lighter weights [*the younger men*]". He introduced another prize for the first to reach 90 years. Who won this does not seem to have been recorded but the race for the cup for the last Old Contemptible took nearly 30 years. Robert Finch won it in 1985, at the age of 91. He certainly earned his award as not only did he survive the battle of Mons, he also went through Passchendaele, Neuve Chapel, Lens, Loos and Arras before being blinded on the Somme in 1916. Alan Nichols did not even run him close. He died in 1959.

Chapter 7

'A Byword for the Blind, at Home and Overseas'

'Throughout the Empire'
(Title of the St Dunstan's Annual Report in 1921)

The St Dunstan's Annual Report of 1921 began with Sir Arthur's account of the move from Otto Kahn's St Dunstan's Villa to another building dedicated to a saint. This time it was St John's Lodge on the Inner Circle in Regent's Park, opposite the Royal Botanical Gardens. There was no temptation to change the name of St Dunstan's. It had by now become a byword for work for the blind. This great house was built on what had been the site of a projected great palace for the Prince Regent, (later George IV), and it had since been the home of the Marquess of Wellesley and the Marquesses of Bute. During the war, St John's Lodge was used as a Red Cross Hospital.

Otto Kahn had asked for his house back after a loan of five years. Sir Arthur spoke of St Dunstan's "deep debt of gratitude" to the Kahns, "who for so long gave St Dunstan's and its beautiful grounds for their use and enjoyment. St Dunstan's has been the training centre for nearly 2,000 men; a fact which I am sure will mean more to Mr and Mrs Kahn than could any expression of thanks".

The move entailed converting the large and lofty rooms of St John's Lodge, including the ballroom, into office accommodation for the various specialist departments of what had by now become a great enterprise. New workshops were built in the grounds and it was proudly reported that there was no interruption to the work of training during the move. The trainees soon learnt their way about their new home and conveniently the grounds stretched down to the lake, where the rowers enjoyed their sport.

* * * * *

The title of the 1921 St Dunstan's annual report, 'Throughout the Empire' was well justified. There were by then 15 'colonials' in training at the new centre. So far, 63 Canadians, 70 Australians, 10 South Africans and 20 New Zealanders had already completed their training, as farmers, masseurs, mat-makers, and shorthand typists, and returned home.

A report from Lillian Vintcent in South Africa described how well the blinded soldiers re-settled in that country were succeeding. Charles and Lillian Vintcent had made themselves responsible for the after-care of St Dunstaners in South Africa. This was a matter of great importance as these men were now so far away from St Dunstan's in London. The Vintcents had originally taken an interest in the war-blinded in London, where they had been living during the war, and had befriended their compatriots among the trainees in Regent's Park. When they returned to South Africa in 1918, they volunteered to set up a committee to raise funds for St Dunstan's in South Africa and Rhodesia and to establish an after-care service there. The committee was formed in 1918, and Charles Vintcent became Chairman while Lilian acted as Honorary Secretary. They found a powerful ally in a blind member of the South African parliament, Walter Bowen, who was himself a St Dunstaner, and the first South African soldier to be blinded.

Bowen had been serving as a sergeant when he was wounded at Ypres in 1917, but he was undeterred from his ambition to become a barrister and he studied at Cambridge University. He left university with BA and LLD degrees and was called to the Bar in London in 1920. Bowen returned to South Africa two years later, where he became an advocate of the South African Bar. In 1929 he was elected to the South African Parliament and remained an MP until his death in 1948. As well as providing support for the fledgling St Dunstan's South Africa, Bowen was instrumental in the establishment of the South African National Council for the Blind.

* * * * *

After-care organisations on the St Dunstan's model were set up in the other dominions, in many cases under the direction of former St Dunstaners. Two of the first Canadian St Dunstaners to return to their homeland were

Alexander Viets and Edwin 'Eddie' Baker. Viets had worked for the Imperial Life Assurance Company in Canada before he went to war. He left St Dunstan's in 1916 to return to his home in Nova Scotia. There he spent some months selling newspaper and magazine subscriptions with such success that he was taken on to the sales team at his old employer. After a difficult start, he became one of their most successful representatives. Eddie Baker also came to Toronto to join the Hydro-Electric Power Company, where he dealt with reports of faults, arranged repairs and drafted correspondence.

The two St Dunstaners found that there was a great deal lacking in provision for blind people in the city. In 1917 Alexander Viets wrote to *St Dunstan's Review*: 'The care and education of the blind in Canada generally and in Toronto in particular, is in a very bad state at present, more especially as it concerns the adult blind; and we think it will be through the returned blinded soldiers that considerable interest will be aroused, and when the war is over a lot of good can be done in our own line in educating and interesting the general public'.

Viets's words were prophetic and it was through the efforts of two returned Canadians – himself and Eddie Baker – that progress was made. They had the support of a Toronto business man, Lewis Wood, in their pioneering work, which was very quickly crowned with success. In March 1918 a Dominion Charter set up the Canadian National Institute for the Blind. Sir Arthur Pearson was the Honorary President and the headquarters in Toronto was named Pearson Hall.

Baker became responsible for the settlement and after-care of all Canadian blinded ex-servicemen when he was appointed Secretary of the Blinded Soldiers Department of the Invalided Soldiers Commission of Canada in June 1918. At the same time, the Canadian equivalent of St Dunstan's was set up under the title The Sir Arthur Pearson Association of War Blinded. By this time Canadian St Dunstaners numbered 170, their training at Pearson Hall was supervised by other St Dunstaners and Canadian VADs who had returned from England. Eddie Baker gave up his job with the Hydro-Electric Power Company to take on his new responsibilities, which widened to include the civilian blind in 1920, when he became Managing Director of the Canadian National Institute for the Blind. Baker's service to war-blinded Canadians was recognised in 1935, when he was made Officer of the Order of the British Empire.

* * * * *

In New Zealand at the time of the First World War there was only one organisation concerned with blind welfare and it was primarily a local one. The Jubilee Institute for the Blind in Auckland, mainly an education establishment, had no facilities for occupational retraining. A St Dunstaner was to change all this. Clutha Mackenzie was blinded in 1915, while serving at Gallipoli with the Wellington Mounted Rifles. He was the son of Sir Thomas Mackenzie, then New Zealand High Commissioner in London and a former Prime Minister of New Zealand. After completing his training at St Dunstan's Clutha stayed on in London with his father until the end of the war. He married a VAD, Doris Sawyer, and ran a fortnightly magazine for the New Zealand Expeditionary Force.

On his return to New Zealand, Clutha brought with him the ideals of blind welfare that he had learned from Arthur Pearson. He joined the Jubilee Institute and demonstrated the need for the expansion of its activities, receiving every encouragement to raise funds for this purpose. He succeeded only by great personal effort, involving travelling the country on horseback to raise money through local activities. He was appointed Director of the Jubilee Institute, which later became the New Zealand Institute for the Blind.

Clutha Mackenzie became a Member of the New Zealand House of Representatives in 1921 and received a knighthood in 1935. When the Second World War came he was in India on holiday and St Dunstan's asked him to stay on for a short while to set up a fundraising organisation there. Once again he found no provision for the training or welfare of blind people – not even the war-blinded. During the First World War, faced with the Indians' traditional fatalistic approach to blindness, St Dunstan's had balked at attempting to provide anything similar to its efforts at Regent's Park. Instead grants were made to blinded Indian soldiers, which could be used to provide pensions.

However, Clutha Mackenzie found these ex-service pensioners unoccupied and unhappy, which inspired him to set up a training centre. It was established in 1943 in a former POW and internment camp provided by army authorities at Dehra Dun in United Provinces (now Utter Pradesh). He stayed throughout the war and by 1945 more than 70 men had passed through Dehra Dun, including some English soldiers. At the same time Clutha Mackenzie was conducting a survey of the blind population in India. The Indian Government had requested St Dunstan's to allow him to spend half his time on this enormous task – the blind population in India was estimated at around a million at the time. This resulted in plans for welfare services for blind people in India after the war. Sir Clutha's services to Indian blind people also included the development of a system of Braille reading and writing for the languages of the sub-continent, which led to his appointment as Braille Consultant to UNESCO and the spread of the use of Braille throughout Asia and Africa.

Two other casualties of Gallipoli are credited with the beginnings of the Australian equivalent of St Dunstan's, Elmer Glew, inevitably known as 'Sticky', and Charles Hill, who came to Regent's Park within days of each other in August 1915. Charlie Hill trained as a poultry farmer with the intention of settling in Britain, but he suffered from rheumatism and was advised to return to Australia and a more suitable climate.

There he found no after-care service and total disbelief that a blind man could run a poultry farm. He proved the latter wrong by his own exertions and his example led to other blinded Australians making their way to England and St Dunstan's. In New South Wales, Hill pioneered an after-care facility, while Elmer Glew was responsible for a similar service being set up in Victoria. He had returned to Melbourne as a fully trained masseur. Like Hill he found some scepticism among his compatriots and the Australian Massage Association insisted on a further six months training before awarding him their diploma.

So in Australia separate after-care committees were established. There was further St Dunstan's influence in Adelaide, where the Blinded Soldiers Association of South Australia had the assistance of the Misses Gurner, Stirling and Went, all former members of St Dunstan's VAD staff in London. All the committees worked in co-operation with the Australian Red Cross. Later a federal organisation, the Australian Blinded Soldiers was set up, known as Blinded Soldiers of St Dunstan's Australia from 1973.

In this way the name St Dunstan's spread through all the major countries of the Commonwealth. It is a reminder that the 'colonials' of the First World War and their successors from the Empire of the Second made their contributions and their sacrifices to victory over the enemy in war and over blindness in peace.

Chapter 8

The King is Dead,
Long Live the King!

'The noble benefactor of the blind'
(Queen Alexandra speaking of Arthur Pearson, after his death in 1921)

U nder the leadership of a man as dynamic as Pearson, St Dunstan's
had quickly become a paternalistic organisation. Pearson was
unused to any kind of suggestion that a voice from within the
'family' might wish to be heard. However, in 1921, one voice spoke up, that
of Edmund Toft, a 26-year-old masseur and osteopath, blinded while serving
with the 7th Royal Sussex Regiment in 1916. When Toft suggested forming
an association of St Dunstaners, Pearson's pride was stung.

Pearson immediately organised a postal poll of St Dunstaners on the
topic. The response was an overwhelming vote for the status quo, with 1,117
of 1,201 against the formation of an association, only 12 for. Edmund Toft,
however, was not satisfied. He felt that the aims of his suggested association
should have been explained and he wrote to Ian Fraser, then Director of
After-Care, asking for a letter to be published in the *St Dunstan's Review*. 'I
wish to say that the advocates of this association do not wish to interfere in
any way with the existing organisation of St Dunstan's', wrote Toft, 'but
rather do they want to assist in every possible way the After-Care in its very
difficult task'.

Fraser brought the matter back to the committee, and once again
members were unanimous in the opinion that St Dunstaners 'had shown so
pronounced a disinclination towards forming any association other than the
existing After-Care Organisation that no good purpose could be served by
re-opening the question'. There the matter rested but there were no ill

feelings. Toft went on to a successful career as a masseur and osteopath with a West End practice. He died in 1941 in the service of his fellow St Dunstaners, working as a massage instructor at Church Stretton, the wartime training centre. Toft's initiative could be described as a little local difficulty, but amidst the wider problems of St Dunstan's and the National Institute for the Blind, Sir Arthur Pearson died.

He was discovered drowned in his bath on 9 December 1921. At the inquest, Naomi Glennie, head parlourmaid, told the coroner that she had called Sir Arthur with a cup of tea at 7.15 am. He had enquired about the weather and given instructions as to the suit he planned to wear that day. When he failed to come down to breakfast at his accustomed time, his secretary Amy Campbell went upstairs to look for him. She found him lying face downwards in the bath. His son, Sir Neville, described how his father was lying in the bath with his head under the water, which was discoloured with blood. Sir Neville also noticed blood on the fan-shaped nozzle of the tap. Sir Neville said in evidence that his father had been to the theatre the night before, that he had seen him on his return at about 11 pm and that he was in good spirits. The coroner recorded a verdict of 'accidental causes'. It was sad and ironic that the man who had led so many blinded ex-servicemen to lives of independence should die in a domestic accident.

In his 55 years of life Pearson had built up a press empire and left it behind to build up the National Institute for the Blind and, the work he probably would have most wished to be remembered for, the creation of St Dunstan's. His energy was legendary – Joseph Chamberlain had nicknamed him 'the Hustler'. How much Pearson was admired and respected was shown by the spate of tributes in the press and by the public response to his funeral on 13 December.

The service at Holy Trinity Church, St Marylebone, was packed with a congregation that, of course, included many St Dunstaners. The King was represented, as was Queen Alexandra, who had sent two telegrams of condolence to Lady Pearson. Officials of St Dunstan's and the NIB were present, together with representatives of societies for the blind from all parts of the country. A crowd of thousands stood silently outside the church and in the surrounding streets during the service. At Hampstead Cemetery nearly 3,000 people waited for the cortege to arrive. A wreath from Queen Alexandra on the coffin was inscribed in her own handwriting, 'With deepest regret and admiration for the noble benefactor of the blind. Life's race well run, Life's work well done, Life's crown well won. Now comes rest. From Alexandra'.

Another tribute to Sir Arthur came in a letter to a St Dunstaner from Mr E. Mavrogordato, a distinguished journalist, who also acted as a sighted guide for St Dunstaners. He wrote to fellow journalist and St Dunstaner Frederick Martin after the funeral: 'If it had fallen to me to preach his funeral sermon – which heaven forbid – I should have taken for my text the one about Faith, Hope and Charity. He had all three, tho' I doubt if he knew it; none the less that they were not embodied in a form that St Paul would have recognised. I think it was not so much his ability as his charity that made St Dunstan's a success'.

Over 1,500 St Dunstaners came to London to attend Pearson's funeral. They stayed at Regent's Park having travelled overnight from as far as Aberdeen and Plymouth and from all parts of the country, to pay their last tribute to the man they had known as 'The Chief'. It was the tribute he would have appreciated most.

The King is dead; Long live the King! But who was to succeed Arthur Pearson? There was no vice-chairman at St Dunstan's, as no one had expected the need to find a successor to arise so soon. Pearson would have seemed indestructible to those who worked with him. Nor was there any democratic process in place to enable a choice to be made. In theory there was no chairman of St Dunstan's, as Pearson had been Chairman of the Care Committee. The duty to select a new chairman fell upon the remaining members of the Care Committee – Lord Chaplin, Irene Fraser, Captain Vincent Ranger (representing his father, Sir Washington Ranger), Colonel Eric Ball, Henry Stainsby, and Captain Ian Fraser – and a special meeting was quickly called for 12 December 1921.

It is interesting to look at the backgrounds of some of the individuals on the committee. Lord Chaplin was at this time 80 years old. He had been ennobled in 1916, after a political career as a Conservative Member of Parliament, Chancellor of the Duchy of Lancaster and President of the Board of Agriculture. Before her marriage, Irene Fraser had worked with Arthur Pearson as a reader and guide, even before his work for the war-blinded began. She had been Pearson's personal assistant from the start of St Dunstan's, and was as knowledgeable and experienced as anyone on the committee.

As Chairman of the National Institute for the Blind, Sir Washington Ranger was a potential candidate for the St Dunstan's chairmanship. Like Pearson, he was a blind man of immense talent and prestige. He had become blind at the age of 14 and entered Worcester College for Blind Boys, going on to achieve a first class degree in law at Worcester College, Oxford. His firm Ranger, Burton & Frost were the solicitors for the Salvation Army and St Dunstan's. However, by this time he was 73 years old and in poor health. He would retire from the chairmanship of the NIB a year later.

Colonel Eric Ball was wounded in an attack on Loos in 1915 and found himself in the Second London General Hospital with a shattered right arm. In the next bed was a young officer who had been blinded by sniper's bullet just before the same attack. Colonel Ball's interest in the blinded casualties was confirmed when he met Arthur Pearson, who was visiting the young officer. Colonel Ball joined the committee and was involved with St Dunstan's until his death in 1951. He also served in the London County Council and with the Territorial Army.

Henry Stainsby began working for the blind in 1880, when he joined the Birmingham Institution for the Blind. He became General Superintendent and helped to formulate the Braille shorthand system. Stainsby was an innovator in placing blind people in office work and telephony. With the assistance of Alfred Wayne, he devised a Braille shorthand machine and the Stainsby-Wayne Braille Interpointing Machine, which became the main writing machine for blind people for over half a century. As Secretary-General for the Executive Council of the then British and Foreign Association for the Blind, he was recruited by Pearson to establish the means of helping blinded soldiers and was heavily involved in the founding of St Dunstan's. The last member of the committee was Ian Fraser, and also in attendance were Ernest Kessell, Treasurer, and Ellen Chadwick Bates, Secretary.

Finally, Sir Neville Pearson was invited to chair the meeting. He was 23 and had served in the First World War, having been commissioned in the Royal Field Artillery straight from school in 1917. Since the war he had been working in the Pearson publishing businesses. All the speakers were very aware that this was an historic occasion and chose their words carefully. Pearson began by urging his listeners to do all they could to carry on his father's work. He also hoped that the name Pearson should still be associated with St Dunstan's, although because of his lack of experience, he would not be seeking nomination. Instead, he told the committee that, if they wished, his mother would accept the office of President, "the titular head of the organisation".

This brought Sir Neville to the point and he was almost brutally blunt in discussing the possibility of Sir Washington Ranger assuming the chairmanship: "Sir Washington is now getting towards the sunset of this days and I do not feel it would be fair to add to the burden of his declining years by asking him to assume the responsibility of the management of St Dunstan's". Sir Neville then referred to his father's regard for Ian Fraser and hope that Fraser might succeed him, concluding: "He is not very old in years but neither am I. Perhaps this is the time when young men are given greater responsibility?"

Understandably, with his long association with the NIB, Henry Stainsby was disappointed that Sir Washington was unable to take on the chairmanship. He was willing, however, to support the proposal that Ian Fraser be appointed. Lady Pearson was duly appointed President; Ian Fraser as Chairman; Sir Washington Ranger as Vice-President; and Sir Neville as Vice-President and Treasurer

Colonel Ball paid a tribute to Irene Fraser, showing that her presence was an important factor in what was a brave decision for the time: "He will, I am sure, have the assistance of Mrs Fraser who had been associated with Sir Arthur Pearson for many, many years. We all know what an extremely tactful, amiable and capable woman Mrs Fraser is, and she will be of immense help to Captain Fraser in the work which I hope he will undertake". Fraser accepted with due humility. The young lions were taking over, yet through the confidence shown in them by much older men, whose long experience not only of the blind world but also of the wider world, might have been expected to prejudice their decision.

Ian Fraser could have been seen as a risky choice, as he had no experience outside the army and St Dunstan's. Like his new Vice-President and Treasurer he went straight from Marlborough College to the Royal Military College, Sandhurst at the age of 17. On 23 July 1916 he was serving with the King's Shropshire Light Infantry in the Battle of the Somme when he received the head wound that cost him his sight. What he did have in 1921 was all he had learned over nearly five years of working under Arthur Pearson, supporting him on committees, deputising for him and becoming, in effect, Pearson's second-in-command. In February 1917 Fraser had been a St Dunstaner for less than a year when Pearson wrote to his mother to say, 'I have had long talks with Ian lately, and have decided to train him up to assist me in working for the benefit of the blind.'

Ian Fraser did not bury himself in his work for St Dunstan's. In 1921 the Committee of the Blinded Soldiers and Sailors After-Care Organisation (as it had become known in June 1920), approved his running in the London County Council elections as Municipal Reform candidate for North St Pancras. In 1922 he was returned with a majority of over 2,000, unseating a Progressive Socialist member whose party had held the seat for 25 years.

From this platform Ian Fraser moved higher in public life, becoming Conservative Member for North St Pancras in 1924. His maiden speech on 2 April 1925 was on the subject of conditions of employment of ex-service civil servants. The *Daily News*, reported the speech: 'The House of Commons was much impressed last night by the maiden speech of Captain Ian Fraser, Chairman of St Dunstan's. Captain Fraser has a fine voice and presented his case so lucidly in favour of the Treasury agreement on the employment of ex-servicemen that it was hard to believe that he was speaking without a note'.

Over his 34-year parliamentary career, Fraser maintained his interest in the welfare of ex-servicemen and women, blind and sighted. In the Commons, and later as a Life Peer in the Lords, he campaigned consistently for improvements in war pensions. But all this was to come. In the meantime the two young ex-servicemen were preparing to lead St Dunstan's in new directions and through some difficult times.

* * * * *

In 1922, their first year in office, Fraser and Neville Pearson made an important decision to amalgamate the Care and Aftercare Committees at St Dunstan's and incorporate them as a limited company. The Certificate of Incorporation of St Dunstan's was signed by the Registrar of Joint Stock companies on 30 April 1923. The charity now had a constitution like that of an ordinary company, except that the executive council members, governors and members had the roles of directors and shareholders. In the Annual Report of 1922/23 Fraser pointed out that incorporation offered, 'many administrative advantages and strengthens the basis upon which St Dunstan's is to be governed...it conforms to the ordinary practice adopted by most of the leading charities in the country'.

These changes provided a basis of sound and effective management, which has continued to the present day. The chairman presides over a council of around 15 or 16 members and they take all major decisions. In addition some 160 or 170 governors and members are appointed in recognition of valuable services to the charity. They are responsible for approving the annual report and accounts, for re-electing members of the council and for approving constitutional changes.

What had begun as a sub-committee of the National Institute for the Blind, expected only to last for the duration of the First World War, was now a corporate body able to look ahead for the welfare of blinded ex-servicemen and women who would be admitted for many years to come. The incorporation recognised that St Dunstan's was not only here to stay, but also that its remit was expanding. In June 1922 in addition to blinded soldiers St Dunstan's became responsible for 'sailors, airmen, and other persons blinded in or as a consequence of the Great War of 1914-1919 or in any other war or war-like operations'. The charity's new constitution extended the word 'blinded' to 'all cases in which sight has been so impaired that special care and training are required'.

The use of the words 'any other war or war-like operations' were soon proved necessary after an incident in Galway described as an outrage, even in the situation of escalating violence taking place in Ireland at that time. In March 1922, four masked men entered a hospital, St Bride's Home in Galway, where they shot three patients as they lay in their beds. The three men were all members of the Royal Irish Constabulary. Two sergeants were killed outright, while the other man, 29-year-old Constable Patrick McGloin, survived badly wounded and blinded. Under St Dunstan's new remit, McGloin was admitted in July 1922. He had been shot in the right thigh, arm, leg and head, and totally blinded. Another Irish policeman, 30-year-old Constable Thomas Ashe, blinded by shrapnel from an explosion, joined him in September 1922.

Both men went on to live successful lives as blind men. Patrick McGloin returned to Ireland where he ran a poultry farm and kept cattle. He married in 1926 and raised two children before he died in 1967. Thomas Ashe remained in England. Initially he ran a small cornershop with his wife. When the Second War came he re-trained and became one of the pioneering older St Dunstaners who took up factory work, opening the way for hundreds of young men blinded in the Second War to work in open industry alongside sighted colleagues.

Patrick McGloin and Thomas Ashe were the first of many blinded casualties, soldiers and policemen, to come to St Dunstan's after being caught up in the terrorist attacks that have taken place in Ireland.

Chapter 9

Government Inquiry

'Nothing can compensate him
for the loss of his sight,'
(St Dunstan's Council writing generally of the blinded soldier
to the Department of Health, 1924)

The 1920s were a stormy decade for St Dunstan's. Part of this storm brewed in the Advisory Committee on the Welfare of the Blind, established in 1917. Arthur Pearson had been among its members, together with 14 other prominent people in the world of blind welfare. Within a year the committee had unanimously resolved to establish a central agency for collections for organisations for the blind through the National Institute for the Blind. This could have been the first step towards Sir Arthur's aim to consolidate welfare for the blind nationally, but as we have already seen, this foundered at the first attempt.

The wide diversity of fundraising agencies and organisations serving the civilian blind was firmly established, but in the early 1920s their representatives on the Advisory Committee were united in their objections to St Dunstan's appeals activities, believing that too large a percentage of funds was going to too few.

Also, under the Blind Persons Act of 1920, local authorities were responsible for 'promoting the welfare of blind persons ordinarily resident within their area'. To carry out this obligation it was necessary for them to trace the blind people in any local area, including St Dunstaners whose welfare needs were already covered by the St Dunstan's national after-care service. Local blind agencies began to write to St Dunstan's for the names and addresses of war-blinded men living in their areas. Alarm bells rang in

Regent's Park. Stalling replies were sent and legal advice was sought. Ian Fraser feared that giving the addresses of St Dunstaners would make it easier for the Ministry to urge co-operation with civilian organisations.

Enquiries became official on 27 February 1923, when E.D. MacGregor of the Ministry of Health, which was responsible for the Advisory Committee, wrote to Ian Fraser asking for names, addresses and occupations of war-blinded men practising occupations in their own homes. He also asked if St Dunstan's supplemented their earnings and for an estimate of the cost of their supervision. Would it not be more economical, MacGregor wrote, 'to attach these people to properly organised local Home-Workers Schemes?' The words, 'properly organised', seemed to betray a certain bias in the approach of the Ministry of Health and encouraged Fraser to develop a siege mentality, which he maintained throughout his chairmanship.

St Dunstan's reply was lengthy and uncompromising, arguing that local authorities had a duty to act where there was need, yet St Dunstaners had no need of help. MacGregor's words on attaching St Dunstaners to 'properly organised Home-Workers Schemes' were taken up. This 'could not be done more economically, as St Dunstan's staff understand the problem as new people could not' and all war-blinded throughout the UK received the same service. Finally, on the crucial subject of appeals, St Dunstan's asserted that local authorities would have to raise funds to take on this additional work, diverting money away from St Dunstan's. The subject of appeals was a theme that Ian Fraser echoed over the years, but on this occasion it was dragged in unnecessarily and not very diplomatically. It cannot have helped St Dunstan's case in what was to become a serious attack on its efficiency and even its existence. Sure enough, MacGregor's Advisory Committee took a grave view of the contents of the letter and passed it to the Ministry of Health.

These events unfolded against a background of political turmoil that saw three general elections in two years and three Ministers of Health. When the situation first arose in February 1923, Neville Chamberlain was the responsible minister. He became Chancellor of the Exchequer in August and was succeeded by Sir William Joynson-Hicks. The Prime Minister, Stanley Baldwin, called a snap election in January 1924, and lost. The Minister of Health in Ramsay MacDonald's new Labour administration was John Wheatley, a former miner with long experience of local government in Glasgow. However, Wheatley's tenure lasted only nine months. By November 1924, Baldwin was back with the Tories and Neville Chamberlain became St Dunstan's main inquisitor – seemingly by choice! He was offered the Chancellorship again, but opted instead for the Ministry of Health.

The man who stayed at his desk all through was Sir William Arthur Robinson, Secretary, Ministry of Health, a career civil servant. In December 1923, he wrote to Ian Fraser, informing him that the minister had been told that St Dunstan's was collecting a disproportionate amount of money from the public for a limited number of blind persons. There were doubts over economy in the use of funds and over St Dunstan's degree of co-operation with other agencies interested in welfare of the blind.

It took nearly six weeks for St Dunstan's to draft its reply, and by this time John Wheatley was the Health Minister. St Dunstan's Council pointed out that the public recognised that the war-blinded had a special claim on their generosity and that if they gave to St Dunstan's they intended the money to be spent on the war-blind, not on the civilian blind. If St Dunstaners were better provided for then it was because the appeal was a special one in the eyes of the public, who felt that 'nothing can compensate him [*the blinded soldier*] for the loss of his sight'.

The letter contested the charge that St Dunstan's work was prejudicial to the interests of the blind in general, claiming that the organisation had done a great deal to arouse the public conscience on blindness and shown how this could be carried out. As to administration expenses: 'To what other institution can it be compared? There is no other that does so much for its men'. The reply was backed up with financial and statistical evidence.

In September 1924, Robinson informed the Minister, John Wheatley, that the Advisory Committee on the Welfare of the Blind wanted to include a formal attack on St Dunstan's and a demand for a full public inquiry in its annual report, alleging extravagance, lack of co-operation, and unnecessary appeals. Wheatley agreed, but asked Robinson to inform Queen Alexandra's Private Secretary. Queen Alexandra, of course, was the Patron of St Dunstan's. Another General Election loomed and the report was delayed. There was also the feeling that 'Queen Alexandra's name should not be bandied about in public controversy'. Instead, Robinson advised St Dunstan's to agree to an inquiry.

The aftermath of the election found Neville Chamberlain back in office as Minister of Health. Robinson briefed him on the case against St Dunstan's, commenting 'St Dunstan's reply of 5 February, 1924 [*is*] a document which, if published, would, I think, evoke considerable sympathy, though it has had no effect on the Advisory Committee'. The matter was a delicate one, he said, and it was complicated by the fact that Ian Fraser was now a Member of Parliament, and so Robinson suggested that the Minister of Health should meet Fraser to request an inquiry.

St Dunstan's responded with shock and resentment towards the 'allegations of impropriety' made by the Advisory Committee and asked the Minister to meet with members of the St Dunstan's committee. On 17 March, a deputation from St Dunstan's presented itself at the Ministry of Health. The members were: Major J.B. Cohen, MP, a disabled soldier in a wheelchair, Ian Fraser, Colonel Eric Ball and William G. Askew, St Dunstan's Business Manager.

Answering Fraser's opening question as to the purpose of the inquiry, Mr Chamberlain said he had in mind that the investigation should be made in order that the paragraph alleging extravagance and impropriety might, if possible, be expunged from the report of the Advisory Committee before publication.

The meeting soon became heated, as the minutes reveal:

'Chamberlain - What have you to fear from an inquiry?

Fraser - With all respect are you not suggesting that because our constitution is strong we should take nasty pills?... Even though it will not hurt us, why should we be forced to take them?

Chamberlain - You always come back ... to ignoring the facts of the situation, you cannot help it!

Fraser - Is it impossible for you not to judge between our case and the Advisory Committee's case and say that you are impressed by the fact that it is not their business?

Chamberlain - No, I cannot say so.

Fraser - It is impossible?

Chamberlain - Absolutely.

Fraser - Is it their business to seek to decentralise us possibly? They have no jurisdiction over us.

Chamberlain - As an Advisory Committee on the Blind I think they are entitled to say what they think ... I am not going to take their statement as it stands any more than I should accept your denial of it as it stands without having made an investigation of my own.'

The situation needed cooling and an inquiry had become inevitable. It was confirmed that the investigation would be kept within the Department of

Health. Fraser's colleagues were recognising the inevitable. If St Dunstan's refused to co-operate, then the Advisory Committee's damning report would be published. The meeting closed with emollient words from Chamberlain, accepting that St Dunstaners, having lost their sight fighting for their country, were in a different position from the civilian blind. Nevertheless there was iron beneath the velvet as he warned that if St Dunstan's did not accept any recommendations made by the investigation then the report might be made public.

Fraser wrote to Chamberlain formally accepting the inquiry. He still sounded defiant, making the point that there would be no need to substantiate the allegation that more generous allowances were made to St Dunstaners than to the civilian blind: "We admit it and we are proud of it, and shall continue this policy as long as we are able". Nor would St Dunstan's combine or co-operate further with civilian blind charities.

The committee of inquiry was set up under the Chairmanship of Brigadier-General Sir William Alexander, MP. Sir William was a regular soldier who had served through the war and held high positions in weapons and aircraft production. The committee commenced its work in June 1925 and heard evidence from members of the Advisory Committee, the Ministry of Health, the London County Council, the Ministry of Pensions, Ian Fraser, W.G. Askew and Colonel R. E. Bickerton, St Dunstan's ophthalmologist.

The resulting report was critical of St Dunstan's, even severe. Compared with other blind institutions, such as the Birmingham Institution and the London Society, the committee judged that St Dunstan's employed too many staff, particularly in appeals and publicity, and that salaries were unduly high. St Dunstan's appeals were criticised as 'committed to a policy of unknown magnitude in the event of a new war'. In this the committee showed less foresight than St Dunstan's. There was still the greater part of a half-century of armed strife to come.

Ian Fraser came under specific criticism for representing the Advisory Committee as 'trade competitors' to whom St Dunstan's should not share 'for the benefit of the civilian blind, what they considered to be their own ideas'. The committee ended the report with this summary:

'1. That the criticisms of the Advisory Committee, so far as they related to financial administration, had justification and whilst considerable reductions in expenditure have been effected, there is still room for further economies.

2. That while there is no evidence to prove that the large collections of St Dunstan's affect detrimentally other charities for the blind, St Dunstan's is still obtaining more money from the public than its reasonable needs demand.

3. That the attitude of St Dunstan's in deliberately avoiding co-operation with other blind charities and with the two Government Departments concerned in the welfare of the blind is regrettable and not conducive to efficiency.

4. That although the position of the 130 men rejected by the Ministry of Pensions and admitted to St Dunstan's is anomalous, the pensions already granted to them by the charity should not be withdrawn. In future, however, the right of admission to St Dunstan's should be restricted to men who have qualified for a State Pension.'

This was not welcome reading for those leading St Dunstan's, but there were some small chinks of light in paragraph four. This was the acceptance of the continuance of the organisation's work implicit in the strictures on admissions. Meanwhile St Dunstan's had put together a reply that recalled Arthur Pearson's legacy and the tradition of service to St Dunstaners: 'To keep their bodies and souls together at the smallest possible cost was, in a sense, the antithesis of his published aims and appeals'. Chamberlain was assured that economies of every proper kind were being carried out.

Much was made of the claim that comparisons made by the committee were not with organisations doing similar work under similar conditions or with similar objects. St Dunstaners were blinded in the prime of life with ambition still strong in them – they were not children or the aged blind. It was pointed out that, while St Dunstan's was always ready to co-operate, it could not do so where this meant undertaking any activity outside its charitable objects, and these did not include the civilian blind.

Alan Maclachlan, as Assistant Secretary at the Ministry of Health, had been closely involved in the inquiry. His notes were particularly antagonistic to St Dunstan's. He envisaged no more entrants after 1928 and after that there would be very few untrained state pensioners and no difficulty in civilian institutions taking on new cases of war-blinded men. All this was put to St Dunstan's, although not in so many words. Ian Fraser responded by offering concessions to Neville Chamberlain. St Dunstan's would not admit men whose blindness was found by the House of Lords Appeals Tribunals 'not to be attributable to or aggravated by war service'. Steps would be taken by the charity to give up St John's Lodge at Regents Park. St Dunstan's would also calculate what further appeals would be 'justified' and appeals staff and activities would be planned to ensure income was only sufficient to maintain St Dunstan's current scale of assistance.

In December 1926, after more correspondence, the Ministry replied: 'The Minister remains of the opinion that your council should accept some representation on it of the civilian blind charities and should at least make an experiment in the matter of home visiting in a selected area of the country by a civilian blind institution...As, however, your Council do not see their way clear to meet his views on these matters he does not propose to pursue the correspondence further'. What had become something of a poker game was over. Perhaps honours were even, but it had brought about considerable changes in St Dunstan's, creating a more streamlined organisation, which would be of benefit in the lean years to come.

Chapter 10

The 1930s: Recession and Retrenchment

'Blind Heroes hit by the Trade Slump'
(Headline in the *Manchester Sunday Chronicle*, January 1932)

The new St Dunstan's survived the early 1930s recession largely through a more business-like approach following incorporation, and particularly due to the influence of William Askew, appointed Business Manager in 1921. Fraser described Askew as an almost 'mythical indispensable man'.

Starting as Pensions Officer, Askew became Secretary of St Dunstan's in a 36-year career with the charity. When he came to St Dunstan's from the War Office during the First World War, Askew was lame in one leg and ineligible for army service. Nevertheless, he won Arthur Pearson's confidence with his expertise in war pensions. Askew prepared the casework that led to the Pension Appeals Tribunal establishing the precedent that war pensions could be paid for blindness not directly the result of a wound but 'aggravated' by war service, which benefited many hundreds of ex-service people.

Later, the young chairman, Ian Fraser, also came to rely upon Askew. As General Manager, Askew had to tie up the loose ends left over from the Ministry of Health Inquiry: the undertaking to dispose of the lease on St John's Lodge when the Treasury's negotiations with a property developer broke down. The Treasury was willing for St Dunstan's to surrender the existing lease and negotiate a new lease, as previously promised by the developer. New premises for St Dunstan's workshops and stores for the Sales Department were purchased in Raglan Street, Kentish Town. So it turned out, with the added bonus that the Treasury leased part of the property to the Frasers, so that they could continue to live at St Dunstan's Headquarters. They lived in what became known as St Dunstan's Lodge, alongside the offices, for the rest of their lives.

In 1930 Ellen Chadwick Bates, then Secretary of St Dunstan's in Britain, went to South Africa where she became Secretary of the new South African Committee. She took over from Charles and Lillian Vintcent, who had established St Dunstan's South Africa, upon their retirement. In her place William Askew was voted Secretary of St Dunstan's and the office of General Manager was merged with that of Secretary. This meant that Askew would face the problems that came with the 1930s slump and a fall of 25 per cent in St Dunstan's appeals income the following year.

Although Ian Fraser and Neville Pearson decided the drastic steps required for survival, it fell to Askew to implement them. Following the Ministry of Health investigation, Askew had supervised a reduction in staff from 441 in 1923 to 329 in 1929. Then, in 1931 the hard decision had to be taken to make further cuts in staff and reductions in wages. Those earning under £1 per week were exempt, but the majority, earning £52–£300 per annum, found their wages reduced by 2.5 per cent; those earning £300–£400 lost 5 per cent; from £400–£500, 7.5 per cent; and top officials earning over £500 lost 10 per cent. These people were the lucky ones who kept their jobs – nearly half of the headquarters staff were given notice.

Economies fell upon St Dunstaners too. A circular letter explained that grants and loans were to be cut and services reduced. Re-training for changes in employment and help in finding and selecting new properties would be entirely stopped. Worse still, the number of after-care visitors would be significantly reduced.

For the *Daily Herald* of 2 December, 1931, the headline news was a 'St Dunstan's Sensation':

'St Dunstan's has been forced drastically to curtail its work for men who were blinded in the war. A statement that hard times have forced this decision was conveyed to thousands of sightless men and their families yesterday in a letter signed by Captain Ian Fraser, M.P., Chairman of St Dunstan's, who was himself blinded in the war. Many blind men, as a result, will suffer reductions in their pay and allowances varying from £1 to £3 a week, according to the amount of their work and the size of their families.'

Fraser did not rely on his letter alone to explain the situation to St Dunstaners. At meetings and local reunions he spoke to them personally. This resulted in further reports in provincial newspapers on the straits in which St Dunstan's found itself. The Manchester *Sunday Chronicle* brought another aspect of the problem to light on 31 January 1932. 'Blind Heroes hit by the Trade Slump', it announced, with a report pointing out that craftsmen of St Dunstan's found that public demand for their products had fallen steeply. Where, in the past, their surplus goods had been sold through St Dunstan's headquarters, this was also no longer possible.

Through it all St Dunstaners showed great confidence in and loyalty to the organisation and Fraser was able to report that meetings supported the cutback decisions made by the charity. There was a frank explanation of the policy that guided these decisions in the 1932 annual report:

'The responsibilities of St Dunstan's do not decrease as the years pass. On the contrary, middle-age, premature old-age, and aggravation of many conditions arising out of wounds and hardships call for greater individual attention and assistance ... In the year 1931, 31 blinded soldiers have died, but 33 new cases have been admitted ... the actuary has calculated that there will still be 1,300 living [St Dunstaners] in 20 years' time, and some 445 in 40 years' time.'

Referring to the massive drop in collections, the report pointed out that revenue for the year had been helped by some legacy windfalls. Legacies had formed a large part of St Dunstan's income for some years. These were from the wills of a generation that had experienced the war and felt gratitude to those wounded servicemen. Inevitably these benefactions would decline with the passing of the years. 'From this it follows that St Dunstan's must secure the money needed to carry out its plans while memory lives or not at all', urged the report. St Dunstan's would now embark upon a 'policy of endowment', which it was hoped would 'raise the funds necessary for the life-long care of its beneficiaries by 1944 – 25 years from the termination of the War'.

The endowment plan put into operation in 1927 was intended to be monitored every five years, but the national financial crisis of 1931 brought things forward. Prospects were not good, to say the least. An actuarial calculation showed that the fund was £44,000 in deficit and there was an added crisis. Men whose children were born after their disability was incurred received no government pension for their families. Weekly payments to these men were made from the Children Fund, which had been raised during the war years and was now found to be £118,000 short of the amount needed to maintain these allowances.

Part of the legacy windfall was used to shore up the Children Fund but there was still a shortfall of £61,000 and the endowment fund remained in deficit by £44,000. The St Dunstan's Council promised its best endeavours to set this right, 'as soon as circumstances allow', but the deficit would be carried forward through another world war and into the years that followed.

*   *   *   *   *

The ensuing early years of the thirties were a period of rehabilitation; not only for the new St Dunstaners still being admitted, but also for the organisation itself. It was necessary to restore its reputation with the establishment and to recover from the problems left after the depression.

On 20 November 1925 Queen Alexandra died. In her stead the St Dunstan's Council invited the Prince of Wales to become St Dunstan's Royal Patron. The Prince was then at the height of his popularity and he had already assisted the war-blinded with two 'Prince of Wales' picture books of his tours to India and Canada, which had been published and sold for St Dunstan's funds. The Prince of Wales delayed his acceptance while Fraser's problems with the advisory committee rumbled on, and only after his brief accession to the throne as Edward VIII, did he finally become St Dunstan's patron. However, he maintained his interest in the work of St Dunstan's, and delegates to the first St Dunstan's Empire Conference in July 1929 were received in audience by the Prince at St James's Palace.

The conference was important for St Dunstan's as it showed the global extent of the work for war-blinded men. These were the days before the concept of a Commonwealth. No one was embarrassed to describe the delegates as coming from 'our great Empire Dominions'. The delegates discussed matters affecting training, work and welfare of St Dunstaners wherever they lived. As well as their royal reception the delegates laid wreaths at the Cenotaph. Through the conferences that have followed over the years the strong links with the 'colonials' of the First World War and their successors have been conserved.

For the Vintcents from South Africa this was to be their last visit to Britain in office, as they were soon to resign. Their work covered Rhodesia as well as South Africa and they received fulsome praise for their care for the welfare of St Dunstaners in those countries, which was described as 'not surpassed, even by the Mother Country'. Meanwhile, the Empire Conference also speeded up work in Australia. In January 1930, Elmer Glew reported a reunion of St Dunstaners from all parts of Australia and the first moves towards establishing a national organisation for their welfare.

The Prince of Wales was also instrumental in attracting attention to an exhibition of work by disabled ex-servicemen, held at London's Imperial Institute in 1933. Among the exhibits were products made by St Dunstan's home craftworkers. At the exhibition the Prince of Wales learned of the 'Old Bill Fraternity' and decided to join and purchase five shillings worth of goods made by St Dunstaners annually.

Two years later, 1935 saw the celebrations of the Silver Jubilee of Their Majesties King George V and Queen Mary. St Dunstan's held a grand reunion in the Albert Hall. St Dunstaners, with their wives or escorts, were seated at tables set in huge circles around the tiers of the arena. The Prince of Wales spoke warmly of the St Dunstaners he had met in his travels, and praised "the way you who have had this misfortune have settled down to different lives, and have settled down cheerfully, anxious to help yourselves in every possible way". He continued: "I congratulate St Dunstan's, but most of all I congratulate you, and all those men blinded in the War throughout this country and the Empire. I admire your courage, your resource, and the way that you have overcome blindness".

Despite the squabbles with politicians, by 1935 St Dunstan's rehabilitation was progressing based on the public's admiration of St Dunstaners themselves, as expressed by the Prince of Wales. Ministerial confirmation followed in the next year, when St Dunstan's celebrated its twenty-first anniversary. R.S. Hudson, MP, Minister of Pensions wrote a letter of congratulation to Ian Fraser in the warmest terms: 'For many years St Dunstan's has been a household word...In the 21 years of its life St Dunstan's has taken charge of and cared for the blinded ex-servicemen with a completeness and solicitude that is not easily matched...I would say without hesitation that the efforts and success of St Dunstan's on behalf of ex-servicemen have quickened the public conscience in the matter of its obligations to the blind'. It is tempting to wonder whether the Minister of Pensions sent a copy of his letter to the Ministry of Health.

*　*　*　*　*

During the period between the wars Ian Fraser was growing in stature as a public figure. In the General Election of 1929 he had lost his seat in parliament and he resumed his legal studies, and was called to the Bar in 1931, but he was not to practise. With the fall of Ramsay MacDonald's first Labour Government, he won back his seat of North St Pancras in the ensuing General Election.

On his return to Parliament, Fraser enquired about the difficulties encountered by blind voters at the polling station. There were many complaints that the privacy of their voting intentions was being breached. A blind voter currently had to disclose the name of the candidate he wished to vote for to the Presiding Officer and the agents of the candidates and then his ballot paper was marked for him. In 1934 Fraser successfully introduced the Blind Voters Bill, enabling a blind person to take a relative or trusted friend into the polling booth to mark his paper for him.

During his first stint in the House of Commons in 1926, Ian Fraser had helped introduce a bill to allow blind people to have a wireless receiver without a licence. He had been interested in wireless since his schooldays, when he made a crystal set to listen to Morse Code through headphones. Later he became a radio amateur and encouraged other St Dunstaners to take up this hobby. Fraser saw the advent of public service broadcasting as of special importance to the blind: 'So exactly does it fill our needs. The news bulletins are a talking newspaper...Talks are the equivalent of essays and magazine articles...short stories are short stories and plays are plays. Broadcasting comes not only as a wonderful new source of entertainment and instruction, but it helps us to remain informed members of contemporary society'.

Following Fraser's enthusiasm, St Dunstan's agreed to finance wireless sets for every St Dunstaner. In 1933 the council agreed to replace the original crystal sets listened to with headphones, which Ian Fraser described as having 'become a matter of the past', with loudspeaker sets, which were far more comfortable to listen to. This cost the charity £5,000, spread over three years.

Ian Fraser was also a strong advocate of membership of the British Legion. A St Dunstaner, Captain William Appleby, had been one of the founders of the British Legion and many other St Dunstaners were involved at local level in legion branches. However, it was not all plain sailing. To avoid competition, St Dunstan's had agreed with the Legion to give up its own flag day, in return for a four per cent share in the proceeds of the Poppy Day collection. In some eyes this was excessive, and as a result there were resolutions at the 1939 British Legion conference suggesting that St Dunstan's should widen its services to include all blinded ex-service men, even those whose blindness was not due to their service. This was simply not possible, as the funds needed to support existing St Dunstaners and future admissions were already in deficit by £44,000. In the end, the Legion was pacified by the decision to set up a fund for ex-servicemen blind from natural causes, established by Sir Beachcroft Towse, then Chairman of the National Institute for the Blind.

In July 1930, Fraser was invited by the National Institute for the Blind to attend a World Conference on Work for the Blind alongside Clutha Mackenzie, representing New Zealand, and Eddie Baker, representing Canada. The conference was organised by the American Foundation for the Blind, and delegates from 30 different nations attended, presenting papers on such subjects as Education and Training of the Blind, After-Care and Home Workers' Schemes and Pensions. A significant paper was contributed by an American delegate on the employment of blind people in open industry, a topic that was already arousing interest in Britain. A couple of years earlier, at the end of 1929, St Dunstan's had appointed a researcher to investigate the placement of St Dunstaners in industry and similar research was going on at the National Institute for the Blind.

Fraser's own subject was the relationship between the State and blind people – something he could claim close experience of. He opened by saying that the State in many countries only gradually became aware of the needs of blind people. Voluntary effort always came before intervention by the State, he said, giving the example that, in Britain, the first voluntary institution was founded in Liverpool in 1791, while the Blind Persons Act did not become law until 1920. He pleaded for unity and cooperation between State authorities, municipal authorities and voluntary agencies.

At the end of the conference, Ian and Irene Fraser went on to visit Canada, where St Dunstaners had been so important in forming the Canadian National Institute for the Blind. In Toronto the Frasers were invited to a reception at Pearson Hall, where they met 30 St Dunstaners and seven VADs who had worked at Regent's Park. They were received by the Governor-General in Ottawa and met the Prime Minister of Canada and the Minister of Pensions with other Members of the Canadian Parliament. These were all very useful connections to a rising man still only in his thirties and further help towards re-establishing St Dunstan's reputation after the earlier problems. Fraser's rise was recognised in the Birthday Honours in 1934 when Ian Fraser was made a Knight Bachelor 'for services on behalf of the blind'.

Chapter 11

The Quest for Independent Mobility

'With a dog as a guide, one would never feel alone,'
(Letter published in the *St Dunstan's Review* 1930)

In 1931, the General Secretary of the National Safety First Association wrote to the *St Dunstan's Review* asking the views of St Dunstaners on a proposal that they should carry white walking sticks, which might eventually become a recognised sign of blindness. Dozens of St Dunstaners wrote in and of those who responded, the ratio was 20 to one against the idea. Most were reluctant to have any distinguishing mark that set them apart from other men, although they were happy to point out that dark glasses were a sufficient sign of blindness. The aim of St Dunstaners, they said, was to be normal, following the example of their founder Sir Arthur Pearson.

One St Dunstaner pointed out that if the white stick were adopted by the rest of the blind world St Dunstaners would have to fall in line, or become 'a protesting minority'. 'Our answer must be that St Dunstaners are against the proposal', he concluded. 'Whether the rest of the blind world will be for it we do not know. We must wait and see'.

History shows that the white stick did become the symbol of blindness and over the years many St Dunstaners became reconciled and carried one. Many years later a longer and lighter version, the long cane, became a useful tool for independent mobility, still widely used today. Another means of independent mobility, the guide dog, was about to be recognised in Britain in 1930. The resistance shown by St Dunstaners to the idea of a white stick may well have influenced the decision made by St Dunstan's not to take an active part in establishing a training centre for dogs and blind people in Britain.

IN THE MIND'S EYE

Back in 1919 Sir Arthur Pearson had read of the training of dogs in France and was less than enthusiastic: 'It seemed to me that it would need a special brand of dog intelligence if the canine guide were to be brought up to the point that would make him really trustworthy...a dog at the end of a string was apt to remind one a little too much of the blind beggar with his tapping stick and shuffling gait'.

In December 1929, Ian Fraser reported to the St Dunstan's Council on a visit he had made to Germany to learn about their use of guide dogs. The idea was not new. Over centuries dogs leading their blind masters had been a part of the everyday scene often depicted by contemporary artists. Unfortunately, as Pearson had observed, the blind man led by the dog was often presented as a beggar. Yet what was happening in Germany was different. It had begun before the turn of the century, when dogs were trained to seek out the wounded on the battlefield, and the German Red Cross Ambulance Dogs Association, was formed in 1893. The German Army first used dogs successfully in manoeuvres and they proved valuable in the Russo-Japanese War.

Dogs had served throughout the First World War on both sides. In Britain, at Shoeburyness, dogs – mostly Labradors and Alsatians – were trained as message carriers on the Western Front and to carry and lay telephone wires along the front line. In Germany, even while the war was still going on, dogs began to be trained as guides for blind people. In 1916 the first dog was given to a blinded German soldier and by 1919, 539 war-blinded men were guide dog owners. When Ian Fraser went to Germany he found that there were nearly 4,000 guide dogs working there. He also visited an international school for guide dog trainers at Lausanne, in Switzerland, which a wealthy American, Dorothy Harrison Eustis, had established.

Fraser confessed that he had been sceptical, but returned filled with enthusiasm, and hoping to begin an experiment in Britain. The St Dunstan's Council asked Fraser to produce an outline of a working scheme to show the cost of running a training school and the supply of dogs to St Dunstaners. Fraser also tested the water with St Dunstaners by writing a lengthy article, 'The Quest of Independence', for the *St Dunstan's Review* in February 1930. He gave a detailed description of the way in which blind men and women in Germany used their dogs. He described their training and the successes gained in independent mobility. He told his readers that he was making enquiries as to the feasibility of obtaining and training dogs and carrying out an experiment to see if the guide dog could be useful in Britain.

'If we can bring into the lives of British blinded soldiers, or some of them, part of the pleasure which the foreign soldiers I have met secure from the friendship and use of their dog-guides, the effort will have been well worthwhile', he argued. In another article for *The Times* on 18 March, he concluded a little more judiciously: 'We shall have to inquire if there are suitable dogs in England, if they are likely to prove as useful here as on the Continent, and we must consider very carefully whether the ultimate cost of providing them for British blinded soldiers would be justified'.

Interestingly, unlike the white stick issue, many St Dunstaners who responded to Fraser's article were in favour, at least those whose views were quoted in the next *St Dunstan's Review*:

'I would gladly welcome the advent of the dog guide as a means of dispensing with the human.'

'I think that every man who once had a dog guide would never be without one again.'

'With a dog as a guide, one would never feel alone, as a lover of dogs always makes a pal of his dog.'

'My great difficulty is getting enough exercise – my family are not walkers and don't like my going alone. I should not be in the least bit sensitive about being led by a dog.'

Some of those against voiced fears of danger to families of attack by dogs trained to be petted and handled only by their masters, others pointed out that St Dunstaners in employment would have the problem of what to do with the dog during working hours. Another asked what he should do if his dog had a fight!

After considering Fraser's report, the council felt that British blinded soldiers, were 'fortunately better provided for and less in need of a guide than other European blinded men'. They also feared public criticism of the use of dogs for work and noted that the response from St Dunstaners to Fraser's article had been too small, albeit very positive. The costs of such a project would be so considerable that they needed to be much more certain of the scheme and the needs of blinded soldiers before active participation. Fraser's plans were put on hold.

So, for fear of expense and controversy and, possibly, with memories of the Ministry of Health Inquiry in mind, St Dunstan's failed to take up this challenge. This might have changed the whole course of the charity's history by giving it a role to continue even after the last war-blinded man passed away. The finite aspect of work for war-blinded ex-service people was to be blurred by the advent of the Second World War, but it was a frequent reproach from those who criticised St Dunstan's.

In the meantime interest in the work in Germany had been aroused among Alsatian breeders. A former guide dog was brought over from Germany and given to a breeder, Rosamond Bond, who began trying to work the dog. Publicity in the *Liverpool Echo* brought two more people into the picture, Musgrave Frankland, the blind Secretary of the Liverpool Branch of the NIB and Muriel Crooke, Secretary of the local Alsatian League in Wallasey. Also involved were Lady Kitty Ritson and Captain Alan Sington, one of the first visitors to Germany, and Chairman of the fledgling organisation.

The group had raised sufficient funds and established the first dog training centre in Wallasey. The new charity was affiliated to the NIB under the title 'Committee of the Dogs as Guides for the Blind Training Scheme'. William Debetaz, an instructor from the Lausanne school, arrived in 1931 to begin the training of the first four dogs. When that was completed he was able to turn to their prospective owners. The first trainee was Musgrave Frankland, who had been involved almost from the outset. The other three were all St Dunstaners: Allen Caldwell, G.W. Lamb, and Thomas Ap Rhys. The St Dunstaners were not included because of any preference for war-blinded men. Having war pensions simply made it easier for them to spare the time for training than civilian blind people who could ill-afford to lose wages.

St Dunstan's attitude was equivocal. Once again appeals were the contentious point and the two national charities viewed the guide dogs with some suspicion. Appeals became a source of irritation for many years to come. In 1932, on advice from the NIB, the dog guides committee applied for registration as a charity in its own right. The organisation was registered under the title 'Guide Dogs for the Blind'. Thus began what has become one of the most successful charitable appeals in Britain and work for blind people that has given to many thousands independence of movement and the companionship a guide dog brings.

Chapter 12

Talking Books

*'You in turn after Louis Braille have created a revolution
in the blind world',*
(Ian Fraser to Lord Nuffield, 1936)

D espite his total blindness, Ian Fraser maintained his boyhood interest
in radio and set up a workshop in a shed at his home in Regent's
Park. In 1919 he had considered the possibilities of the gramophone
as a means of recording speech instead of music. Now, in the 1930s, that
workshop became the scene of experiments in recording books for blind
readers. Fraser took his dream of making books talk to two of the big
recording companies at that time, Columbia Graphophone and Pathephone.
Records were then recorded at 78 revolutions per minute and ran for roughly
three or four minutes. Recordings were made acoustically, which meant that,
while music did have some semblance to the original sound, the human
voice was badly distorted.

The companies succeeded in lengthening playing time to ten minutes by
slowing down the record, but as Fraser described in his memoirs: 'The
reproduction was vile. The speaker's voice being received by a trumpet
down which the sound waves travelled to a diaphragm making it vibrate.
On the diaphragm was a needle that cut the wax. You had to speak right into
the trumpet to get enough force to cut the wax, and the reproduction was
ruined by resonance'. It was an idea before its time but that time was soon
to come.

In 1925 the recording industry was revolutionised by the invention of
electronic recording. The trumpet was replaced by the microphone and the
sound engineer was born. He was able to control the strength and frequency
of the sound signal that was recorded. This was to be of immense value to

Fraser's experiments in his workshop at St Dunstan's. Bert Cattermole, the Boy Scout who became an employee of St Dunstan's, remembered that workshop and watching the experiments: 'There used to be great slabs of concrete hanging down on wires and these wires ran down to get the speed exactly at 24 revolutions a minute. This was because they couldn't drive the record at 24 revolutions in those days – it was all 78. It used to be a real hotch potch of experiments – everything was Heath Robinson'.

Heath Robinson or not, the experiments gave Fraser hope. By cutting out the bass tones in the voice, they were able to narrow the width of the grooves on the record. This meant that they could be cut at 200 to the inch instead of the normal 100. This doubled the playing time and this was further lengthened to 25 minutes by reducing the speed to 24 revolutions per minute. The next step was to put the experiments on a professional basis. Recording had to be improved. By then, in the United States, a physicist, Lee de Forest, was devising the system for recording sound directly on to film. Could this be an alternative? Also the American Foundation for the Blind was beginning a similar project to record books and there was fruitful co-operation across the Atlantic.

The project in England became a joint one between St Dunstan's and the National Institute for the Blind. As Vice-Chairman of the NIB's Technical Research Committee, Fraser headed the work, which continued in his workshop. The joint project was announced to the press in April 1934. The Gaumont British Company had offered to produce 1,000 feet of film with two tracks of recorded speech, together with a reproducing unit, free of charge. But the joint committee decided against the use of film recording. This was partly due to the fact that special playback machines for readers would have to be developed and the fact that the Americans were by this time committed to discs. If the systems were compatible then recordings could be exchanged. The Americans had already recorded some books at 33 and 1/3 rpm. The Sound Recording Committee urged the Americans to consider using a motor drive that could be varied through 16 rpm to 78 rpm. In the outcome, the British talking book machine had a variable speed regulator, which enabled records to be played at 24, 33, and 1/3, and 78 rpm enabling users to play discs from America as well as music.

By January 1935, future expenditure was estimated at £2,200, to be shared equally by the two organisations. Ian Fraser took to fundraising. He approached Lord Nuffield, who replied that his impression was that 'the majority [of] blind persons who are not in a position to find somebody to read to them, could scarcely be expected to have the education and literary interest...to prefer the recital of a good book to the daily broadcast programme'. Nevertheless, he held out the possibility of a one-off gift of £5,000 to set the scheme in motion. Although grateful for this hope, Fraser was bound to reply to Nuffield's rather poor view of blind people. 'There is a surprising number of blind people who are well educated and take a great interest in affairs and books, but who cannot get enough reading'.

Lord Nuffield decided to make a gift of £5,000 and the Talking Book Library was funded for its first phase, and within days the first five books were chosen for publication. They were: The *Story of San Michele* by Axel Munthe; *Typhoon* by Joseph Conrad; *The Murder of Roger Ackroyd* by Agatha Christie; *The Gospel According to St John*; and *There's Death in the Churchyard* by William Gore.

The next issue was funding the expansion of the library to 1,000 readers. On 22 July 1936, Ian Fraser reported to Lord Nuffield on the way his donation had been spent. He told Lord Nuffield that demand for books necessitated a second recording plant and for the time being they had to restrict membership of the library to 600 readers. Fraser continued: 'You in turn after Louis Braille have created a revolution in the blind world by starting the Talking Book Library for the Blind, and the benefit of this development, in the happiness and future usefulness of a blind community'.

Lord Nuffield undertook to give the project £5,000 a year for seven years. At the same time the Carnegie United Kingdom Trustees had offered £500 a year for three years. This latter was to be used for experimental purposes. The expansion of the Talking Book Library was at last based on a solid foundation. Thanks to continued funding from Lord Nuffield and the Carnegie Trust, the Talking Book Library for the Blind was set firmly on course to grow into the national service it has become. In the first ten years of the Library Lord Nuffield's donations amounted to £47,500, and in later years he gave even more to assist the change from discs to tape recording.

Chapter 13

A Centre Designed for the Blind

'The place is perfect...Every smallest detail seems to
have been thought of ',
(Edmund Toft, 1938)

After the depression of 1931 it might have seemed unlikely that by 1935 St Dunstan's would be considering embarking on a new building project. However, this became necessary when the Brighton Home Committee reported that West House would soon be inadequate to serve the needs of St Dunstaners for holidays, rest care and convalescence.

Matron Adelaide Thellusson was a prominent member of the committee for this project. Her connection with St Dunstan's had begun in 1917, when she joined as a 17-year-old VAD. At only 22, she became Matron of West House, in November 1922. Her long experience must have carried much weight with the council. Writing in the *St Dunstan's Review* in June, 1936, to explain the decision to extend, Ian Fraser said: 'Matron has told me, and many men have confirmed it in talks I have had with them, that some of the stairs and corners in the Brighton Home are difficult to negotiate, and with increasing numbers requiring a change or holiday we have often found we have not enough room'.

St Dunstan's options were to extend West House, to demolish it and put a new building on the site or to build on a new site. A new building on a new site was decided on and Adelaide Thellusson attended the meeting when the decision was made. Sadly she did not live to see the new building completed. She died, still in harness, at West House on 3 December 1937.

74

A CENTRE DESIGNED FOR THE BLIND

West House had the great advantage of being in the centre of things in the Kemp Town area of Brighton. It also had the disadvantage of being an old building not designed for the use of blind people. The opportunity had come to create a building designed specifically to incorporate all that had been learned about the needs of its blind residents. In June 1935 architect Francis Lorne was commissioned to prepare plans and estimate the costs of a six-floor building served by lifts.

There was no site large enough for the building envisaged in the centre of Brighton, but Brighton Council offered the lease of land on the cliffs between Roedean and Rottingdean, not far from the village of Ovingdean. In June 1937 St Dunstan's purchased 12 acres at Ovingdean for £13,000. Soon a skeleton of steel girders was to be seen on the sloping site overlooking the sea. Lorne's conception was a state of the art building in the contemporary, Art Deco style of the 1930s. To conform to the existing building line it was necessary to build at the top of the site some 200 feet above the entrance to the grounds. This left an open, grassy area, around which would be laid paths with guide rails, enabling blind men and women to walk unescorted to take in the sea air. Later this open space would be used for all kinds of sporting activities.

Francis Lorne's design for this concrete and steel-framed building was imaginative. Clad appropriately in sand-coloured bricks, it was to stand at the top of the hill, facing west, looking very like an aeroplane waiting to take off. The fuselage of the aircraft, running east, would be devoted to staff use. The wings, north and south, would provide bedrooms, dormitories and general rooms for St Dunstaners. The cockpit would be the central block with lifts and staircases and, fittingly, on each landing floor-to-ceiling curved windows would create a sun lounge on each floor from the second to the fifth. Windows and light featured prominently in the plans. Including the basement there would be seven floors. Because the building was to be placed along the contours of the slope, rising from front to back, the main entrance was in the basement. Within the building the architect's plans paid great attention to the need for blind people to be able to move around in safety. The principle was that the layout must be so simple that blind people would be able to easily memorise the relationship of the various areas.

Lorne realised that it was important that blind people should have complete confidence that all precautions had been taken to ensure their safety. Some of these were the installation of swing gates at the top of stairways and handrails incorporating signals in the form of studs on the top surface of the rail, indicating which floor the person was approaching. Doors would swing one way only; handles were designed to project as little as possible, and the edges would be padded with rubber. Another innovation was the use of the architect's model as a tactile means of allowing the blind visitor to visualise the building. St Dunstaners could open drawers in the table supporting the model and feel the layout of each floor. Building work began in April 1937 and Lady Pearson laid the foundation stone on 6 September. 'St Dunstan's, Ovingdean', as it became known, finally opened a year later.

Pointing straight out from the front of the building is the chapel. It is crowned with a sculpture carved in reconstructed stone in a style reminiscent of Eric Gill's work on Broadcasting House in London. It depicts a winged figure holding the St Dunstan's torch badge. Facing sternly and defiantly out to sea, the sculpture represents in stone the words of the Founder, Sir Arthur Pearson, 'Victory over blindness'. The chapel accommodates a congregation of 150. A beautiful Art Deco reredos is lit from above by a round skylight in the roof of the chancel. Painted in blue and gold, it represents a dove with outstretched wings. In the nave the pews are made of Australian straight grain walnut. There is a small Compton organ and above the organ loft is a stained glass window, in which stained glass from the Cloth Hall in Ypres is set. This was presented by a St Dunstaner, the Reverend Howard Gibb. Unlike the main building, the chapel has remained virtually unchanged.

By the time the chapel was dedicated in October 1938, St Dunstaners had already moved into the house. When West House closed, as it regularly did, in August 1938, the St Dunstaners did not return. Ovingdean officially opened in October and, writing to St Dunstan's Headquarters, the first occupants warmly praised it:

'It will catch every bit of sun and will put new life into us all.'

'It has been one of the happiest times of my life...A first impression upon entering the hall may be of bewilderment at such a spacious apartment but the lasting impression is the simplicity, but efficiency of every arrangement. Within one hour of entering I was so at home in the ward and dormitory that I felt I must have stayed there on several occasions. Progress in visualising the dining-room, lounge and other rooms on the main floor was not quite so rapid but I found

that frequent use, and a great familiarity with these began to produce that sense of satisfaction which something attempted, something done always brings...I never did enjoy my meals so much as I did last week. It was the constant talk of the table – no complaints.'

'The place is perfect...Every smallest detail seems to have been thought of – the stairs are gentle and easy, and so clear are the indications on the balustrades and the doors, and so alike are the corridors on each floor, that after a few hours the place seemed quite familiar to me ... I was slightly apprehensive as to crossing the main road, but I tested this with another totally blind man. We stood at the Belisha beacon. (an early type of pedestrian crossing) Held out our hands in a commanding manner and both lines of traffic came simultaneously to a stop.'

Edmund Toft, who wrote the last letter, may have safely crossed the busy road that runs along the coast as no doubt many others did. But, in fact this crossing was to make the only dent in the euphoria that greeted the home. In January 1939 there were two accidents in quick succession. In the first, one of three St Dunstaners was knocked down and suffered a broken leg. The second happened at night and no less than seven St Dunstaners and two sighted people were involved, but fortunately only cuts and bruises were incurred. As a result Brighton Council hastened the installation of lighting on two special notices warning of blind pedestrians, which had been delayed. St Dunstaners were informed of the dangers of the crossing and urged to take utmost care. More transport was arranged to avoid, as much as possible, St Dunstaners having to return from Rottingdean by public transport.

To solve this problem, a pedestrian tunnel was dug under the coast road, financed jointly by St Dunstan's and Brighton Council. Sadly, before it was finished, a St Dunstaner died. Sidney Smith, visiting from Northampton, was walking alone on the morning of 27 May 1939, when he attempted to cross away from the pedestrian crossing. He was knocked down and killed. The tunnel was finally opened in April 1940 and from then on no St Dunstaner needed to cross the road. But by then the Second World War had begun.

Chapter 14

The World at War Again

"When the question of the care of casualties of the present war arose, I said, 'Go to St Dunstan's'",
(Sir Walter Womersley, Minister of Pensions, March 1940)

Although it took some time for its significance to be recognised, an event took place on 27 February 1933 that would totally change the world, and with it the situation of St Dunstan's. That night in Berlin the Reichstag, the seat of democratic government in Germany, was burned down. Adolf Hitler, as Chancellor, took this the opportunity to issue decrees suspending all legal guarantees for personal liberty, freedom of speech and the press and the right of assembly. Through the violence of the Nazi Storm Troopers all political opposition was suppressed and Hitler obtained dictatorial powers. The fire was blamed on Communist terrorism and the Nazis seemed implacably opposed to Communism. With the memory of the Russian Revolution still fresh in their memories, European governments were more than ready to give the Nazis the benefit of the doubt. There followed years of increasingly uneasy peace, with many people in this country ready to accept Herr Hitler and to endeavour to co-operate with Germany.

Naturally among ex-servicemen there was the mutual respect that often exists between former opponents even in war. In March 1936, Ian Fraser visited Berlin at the invitation of the German War Victims Care Association, the equivalent of the British Legion. It is interesting that Fraser felt it necessary to justify his visit by referring to views expressed by St Dunstan's new Royal Patron King Edward VIII. While still Prince of Wales, the King had addressed the British Legion Annual Conference commending the idea that ex-servicemen in Britain and Germany should communicate with one another. Fraser attended the two-day German Remembrance celebrations and although he made no reference to this visit in his autobiography *My Story of St Dunstan's*, he gave a full account in the *St Dunstan's Review* at the time. The celebrations began in the Opera House, where around 5,000 people, including representatives from the blind soldiers' organisations of France, Italy and Poland, had gathered. The vast majority of the audience, Fraser observed, were in uniform:

'When Herr Hitler entered everybody rose to their feet and gave him the Nazi salute, after which the National anthem of Germany, Deutschland Uber Alles, the Nazi Party Song, and an old soldier song called I have a Good Comrade were sung. We then went to a big square where the War Memorial is situated. Herr Hitler was the only person who laid a wreath. He then took the salute from some very smart contingents of the German Army, Navy and Air Force. The ex-servicemen did not march by or lay wreaths as they do in England. After this the foreign guests were presented to Herr Hitler, who shook hands with us but did not speak.'

Fraser laid a wreath the next day and, afterwards attended the opening of the Blinded Soldiers' House. All the speeches, except his own, were of a political nature, he told his readers. He passed on to them some of the information he had learned from the 'many courteous friends I made'.

The following year, a group of German ex-servicemen visited St Dunstan's, with two war-blinded men among them: August Matens, leader of the German War-Blinded Organisation and Hans Voigt, District Leader of Hamburg. Then, in July 1938, only four months after the Austrian Anschluss, three St Dunstaners visited Germany taking up an invitation given the year before. They visited two homes for the war-blinded and returned full of enthusiasm for their reception and for the German standards of provision for ex-servicemen. One of the St Dunstan's visitors, D. Maclean, of Brimpton, wrote: 'I have just returned from a memorable visit to Germany. I say 'memorable' because my experience has completely changed my previous views of Herr Hitler...there is no doubt as to the sincerity of the German people to be friends with England, and they are no less sincere in their desire for true peace'.

In some ways Maclean and his fellow visitors were not wrong. Yet they had seen only one face of Germany, and historians have concluded that

Hitler and his Generals hoped to achieve their Lebensraum without going to war with Great Britain. Germany's other face was less appealing and in 1938 plans were well under way in this country to prepare for the possibility of conflict. Britain and France had threatened Germany that any move against Czechoslovakia would lead to war. In September the Czechs were persuaded to hand over the Sudetenland to Germany. Neville Chamberlain believed he had achieved 'Peace in our time' with the signing of the Munich Agreement. However, in March 1939 the Germans marched into Prague and even Mr Chamberlain realised that war was becoming inevitable.

The events leading to Munich had been a full-scale emergency and a dress rehearsal for the plans that St Dunstan's, like so many British organisations, was making ready for war. It was expected that London would be the target for air raids and St Dunstan's staff members were advised that it was likely that all welfare work would be carried on at West House, in Brighton, with Ovingdean accommodating existing St Dunstaners and new admissions, while appeals work would remain in London. However, the intention was to remain at London Headquarters until this became impossible. Meanwhile, the welfare staff were seeking and inspecting lodgings for St Dunstaners and their families who might need rehousing.

Should war break out procedure was clear: a small nucleus of staff was instructed to report for duty, while the rest were asked to remain at home to await instructions. During the period of waiting, they were promised that their wages would be sent by post. At headquarters and at Brighton air raid shelters were prepared and St Dunstan's had its own stock of gas masks for staff who had not received one of their own. All records, files and accounts were safely evacuated to places of safety.

Early in 1938 Ian Fraser met Sir Adair Hore, Permanent Secretary at the Ministry of Pensions, to offer St Dunstan's services to blinded casualties in event of another war. He proposed to 'take care of soldiers, sailors and airmen and other persons blinded in or as a consequence of any war or warlike operations'. This offer would also be made to the Governments of the Dominions. Fraser explained, 'we would educate and rehabilitate them in the general manner in which St Dunstan's has rendered this service to blinded men of the Great War'. The men from a new war would also receive after-care for the rest of their lives. They would be a new generation of St Dunstaners. More than this, St Dunstan's offered to take casualties as soon as the Ministry considered it likely they would be blind or even earlier. For this purpose it was suggested that an operating theatre wing would be created at Ovingdean. Although Fraser wrote that St Dunstan's 'would not wish to become more an eye hospital than an institution for the war-blinded'.

Sir Adair, in a favourable reply, picked up on the words 'other persons' in Fraser's letter, pointing out that large numbers of members of Air Raid Precautions and civilians might be blinded. In his reply, Fraser said he would wish to consult his advisers but also questioned Sir Adair: 'I think you told me in our conversation that the Government had decided that members of the Auxiliary Defence Services, ARP personnel, Air [Raid] Wardens etc...would receive similar treatment to that afforded to members of the Armed Forces? Would you kindly let me know if this is correct?' Sir Adair's hand-written reply was brief: 'The answer to this question was 'yes''. Fraser said he thought that St Dunstan's might find difficulty in distinguishing between different classes of blind person and, this would indeed, create problems later on.

Fraser had also outlined plans for an operating theatre at Ovingdean some time before the outbreak of war: 'one ophthalmic operating theatre, one small general operating theatre, a sterilising room, anaesthetic room, nurses' room, doctors' room and usual offices'. On 3 September the German invasion of Poland brought Neville Chamberlain to announce to the House of Commons: "This country is now at war with Germany. We are ready". St Dunstan's was ready, thanks to the dress rehearsal in 1938 and the plans made earlier that year. The establishment of the War Hospital at Ovingdean was made public in a press release on 25 October. After all that had gone on in the recent past the organisation could not resist an element of self-congratulation:

> *'The Government has paid a signal compliment to the work of St Dunstan's for the war-blinded during the past quarter of a century, by entrusting it with the treatment of serious eye cases in the present war and the training of men thereafter...The Home is capable of taking two hundred patients. A temporary operating theatre is ready and a new and perfectly equipped operating theatre block containing the most up-to-date ophthalmic and general theatre is nearing completion.'*

Financed by a generous gift from Lord Nuffield, the new block was finally built over the garage area and was entered through a walkway created from the North Wing. The plans for this facility laid in the months leading up to the war, even included purchase of steel girders, in case of supply problems in wartime. Although the early days became known as the 'Phoney War', in its first six months the hospital admitted 43 men with severe eye injuries. Happily many of them left with their sight restored by the surgeons.

Sir Walter Womersley, Minister of Pensions, officially opened the theatre wing on 8 March 1940. He said that he was the right man to open the wing as he was himself blind in one eye. His remarks made it clear that, as in earlier centuries when soldiers and sailors, neglected and rejected in peacetime, were valued once more when war came, the coming of another conflict had changed officialdom's attitude to this ex-service charity, publicly at least. "When the question of the care of casualties of the present war arose, I said, 'Go to St Dunstan's', for I knew that St Dunstan's, with its experience and knowledge was the best authority to deal with such a problem".

Although gratified to be back within the government's embrace, Ian Fraser was anxious to emphasise that St Dunstan's status had not changed: 'The fact that the government has entrusted St Dunstan's with this important duty does not affect its status as a voluntary agency. It will remain thus, as always in the past, supported by the goodwill and generosity of the British people'. Fraser also foresaw the need for new buildings at Brighton to accommodate training facilities, which would have to expand to meet the kind of demand experienced in the First World War.

By making it clear that St Dunstan's would continue to appeal for funds, he was reassuring the existing St Dunstaners that the new responsibilities being undertaken would not mean any neglect of the 'First War men', as they soon came to be known. There was still accommodation available for existing St Dunstaners at Ovingdean and their presence was recognised as reassuring for the first young casualties. In June 1940 Ian Fraser, recently elected Member of Parliament for Morecambe and Lonsdale, thanked, as he put it, old St Dunstaners, "Who have gone out of their way to cheer and comfort these lads".

This was not the only way that First War St Dunstaners could contribute. In 1938 Sir Samuel Hoare, had publicly appealed for volunteers to serve in Air Raid Precautions, (ARP). Patrick Garrity, a blind telephone operator who lived in Purley, South London, wrote to Ian Fraser suggesting that St Dunstaners working as telephonists should, in their spare time, volunteer to use their skills at hospitals, fire stations, or town halls in emergencies. Fraser encouraged St Dunstaners in this and, as war approached, many became involved in ARP. The first St Dunstaner to qualify as an Air Raid Warden was Thomas Williams in Sheringham. Later, Charles Durkin was made Head Warden of the Roehampton Estate responsible for the ARP organisation for a community of 5,500 people and commanding 50 wardens. The Deputy Group Controller for Princes Risborough was yet another St Dunstaner, Alec Biggs.

When air raids began, some St Dunstaners became roof-spotters, warning of the approach of enemy aircraft. Factories did not stop work when the sirens sounded their warnings. Operations continued until a spotter stationed on the roof signalled the approach of an enemy aircraft. In poor visibility the sound of an aircraft was often the only way of detecting its presence. A blind man's necessary reliance on his hearing gave him an advantage in these circumstances and some became local celebrities through their ability to identify enemy aeroplanes by the distinctive sound of their engines. Others worked in teams of fire watchers, who dealt with incendiary bombs. You did not need to be able to see to operate a stirrup pump, provided someone else aimed the hose. Later in the war, when the Home Guard was established, some St Dunstaners joined this force, working in the local headquarters. One became the armourer in charge of the rifles, booking them in and out and keeping them clean.

The blackout that was enforced so strictly by the Air Raid Wardens gave St Dunstaners an advantage over sighted friends and relatives. There were many accidents in the blackout, most of them minor, and everyone had their blackout story. One St Dunstaner physiotherapist arrived at his clinic one morning with a significant bruise on his forehead. Asked by a colleague, he explained how it had happened: "I went out with a friend who unfortunately wasn't blind!"

*   *   *   *   *

At a conference on 1 November 1938 with representatives from various government departments a tentative agreement was reached that St Dunstan's would be responsible for the rehabilitation and care of all officers, nurses and men of the armed forces of the Crown, including members of the auxiliary forces. Further, Fraser's suggestion that Ovingdean could be used as a hospital for cases needing medical treatment before training was also taken up. It was agreed that these men would be transferred to St Dunstan's as soon as medical authorities decided that the patient was blind and fit enough to travel.

Further consultations took place with the Ministry of Health, Ministry of

Pensions and with the National Institute for the Blind in June 1939. As a result St Dunstan's remit was widened. Fraser explained that in addition to Air Raid Precautions personnel and special constables, the Ministry of Health had suggested that St Dunstan's should also consider caring for blinded members of the regular Police Forces and Fire Brigades and would be the organisation 'best fitted to train and care for them'. Needless to say, the St Dunstan's Council unanimously accepted this extra responsibility.

St Dunstan's was also looking into the possibility of caring for blinded civilian casualties. Ian Fraser wrote on 13 November 1939, to the Principal Medical Officer for Emergency Hospital and Medical Services, that St Dunstan's constitution (known as its Memorandum and Articles of Association) allowed the charity to 'care for any persons of either sex blinded in or as a result of the Great War or any subsequent war or war-like operation'. Fraser had been wrong in saying that St Dunstan's constitution permitted treating blinded civilians who were not on any kind of war service. There should be no difficulty in having the necessary changes made by the Charity Commissioners, but in the meantime he requested that the Minister of Health enable St Dunstan's responsibilities to be widened.

The Charity Commissioners approved the extension of St Dunstan's objectives on 19 July 1940. From now on St Dunstan's could 'provide for the medical or surgical treatment, re-education, training in one or more trade or trades, settlement and permanent welfare of Soldiers, Sailors, Airmen and other persons including women and other non-combatants blinded in or as a consequence of the Great War of 1914-19 or in any other war or warlike operations'.

This considerable extension of St Dunstan's objectives caused concern in civilian blind circles, particularly within the NIB. The NIB objected to the announcement that St Dunstan's intended to offer full services to civilian volunteers blinded on duty in a list of civil defence duties qualifying for personal injuries pensions from the government. A series of conferences were held and at first Fraser, with the backing of the government, was disposed to persist with the aim to treat, at least initially, all civilians who might be blinded. However, where civilians were concerned, further rehabilitation and re-education would be the responsibility of other voluntary organisations and local authorities.

Chapter 15

Church Stretton

'Stretton was one of the happiest years of my life'.
(Bob Lloyd, St Dunstaner)

Ian Fraser was responsible for finding a safe place for a 'shadow Emergency Hospital and training centre' if Ovingdean should be threatened. Assisted by his wife Irene and their right-hand man William Askew, Fraser started the search for a site with 'room for rapid expansion if necessary...quiet and well away from bomb-targets, yet...on a main railway line so that the men could easily travel home'. They found Church Stretton, a small town in the Shropshire hills, where there was an hotel, the Longmynd, large enough to become the nucleus of a training centre. The hard tennis courts could also accommodate additional huts.

The war had come to Church Stretton in September 1939 in the form of evacuees who swelled the population, and doubled the size of the school, which expanded into the parish hall. The army moved in next, commandeering big houses and hotels, and building huts for their service men and women. The new by-pass around the town also became an army transport depot. Now, St Dunstaners, patients and staff from Ovingdean moved in, arriving at the Longmynd Hotel on 26 August 1940. Ovingdean and West House were closed and the staff from West House moved back to London. Later the two Homes in Brighton were requisitioned by the Admiralty and Ovingdean, along with neighbouring Roedean School for girls, and became HMS *Vernon,* an underwater weapons school.

At about the same time St Dunstan's obtained two other homes. The Concord Hotel, South Promenade, Blackpool, accommodated 30-35 St Dunstaners with staff, and was used as a convalescent and holiday home until 1952. Also, William Ruxton, an American friend of Ian Fraser's, offered the rent-free use of Melplash Court near Bridport. The house was built in the sixteenth century and had once belonged to Sir Thomas More. Ruxton had added a new wing, but the house still retained many of its historic features. For the duration of the war it became the home of elderly St Dunstaners needing permanent residence and those requiring constant bed-care or a period of convalescence. For Melplash a local matron was recruited, Mary Crossley, Assistant Commandant of the VAD. Both the Concord Hotel and Melplash Court, from time to time, also took in St Dunstaners who were bombed out of their homes. Local accommodation for their families was arranged nearby until they could return to their homes or new ones if resettlement was necessary.

The first group of St Dunstaners arrived at Melplash Court by coach, driven by Lawrie Austin. His coach also carried the first St Dunstaners to Church Stretton and, in 1938, he had brought the first arrivals to Ovingdean. Lawrie Austin at that time was working for Albion Motors and was sent to St Dunstan's at Regent's Park to demonstrate a new coach. "The idea was to demonstrate the coach and return to the works but I was offered a job", Lawrie recalled. He was one of the first members of staff at Brighton and in 1940, after delivering his passengers, he stayed on at Church Stretton. "My wife was in London and I was staying in Shrewsbury. It was a bit of a tough time because we couldn't see each other because of the distance and transport was difficult".

Despite the problems of separation so typical of the effects of the war on family life, and shared by other St Dunstan's staff members, Lawrie had some good memories of those days. On one occasion a local farmer needed help with apple picking: "I had to take some of the men to Hope Bowdler (a village close to Church Stretton). These lads were all youngsters in their twenties. They started climbing the trees! One got up a tree, his foot slipped and a branch went up his trouser leg. There was another man with a knife trying to cut him free. We had a job getting them down. They were great fun I was sorry to go into the Royal Air Force and leave them". However, after serving through the rest of the war in the RAF and in the Fleet Air Arm, Lawrie returned to St Dunstan's as Transport Manager. He retired in 1978 after 40 years service. "Every day – although it was the same sort of job – was a different day and what I got out of it was helping someone who is disabled, although I would not call it disabled. They've got a snag that's all and if you can help them to enjoy life a little bit more and help them on their way".

CHURCH STRETTON

Of all the wartime invaders of Church Stretton, it is fair to say the most memorable were the war-blinded men and women of St Dunstan's. A new residential development in the town was named St Dunstan's Close in April 1989 and at that time many residents of the town still had vivid memories of the blinded soldiers.

Just as in Regent's Park 25 years before, a small girl became guide and friend to the new generation of St Dunstaners. Young Pauline was the daughter of Mr and Mrs Trebble, licensees of The Plough, one of a number of pubs in the town favoured by St Dunstaners. She was five years old when they first came, "We used to be packed out with them. We had a piano and they used to like to sing". Later in life, now Mrs Pauline Haycock, she recalled that, like Little Ruby in Regent's Park, she used to guide St Dunstaners:

"From the Longmynd a wire was put across the field so the boys could be independent and one of my jobs was showing them how to use it. I used to take them and put them on the wire and if they were new boys I would have to show them the way up the wire. Lunchtimes they used to wait until I had to go back to school and I would take them. They were going from their workshops which were in the town centre where the fire station is now. They would call in for their lunchtime drink and then when I was ready to go back after my lunch I would take two or three, put them on the wire and they would find their own way to Longmynd or Tiger Hall whichever they were at."

The wire that Pauline Haycock refers to ran all the way down the hill from the Longmynd to the town centre on posts at roughly waist height. As she suggests, St Dunstan's soon occupied other buildings. The army handed over Tiger Hall, which became the hospital, and also gave up nine huts in the centre of the town. Various classes were held in the huts: basket-making; boot repairing; Braille and typing; industrial training; and telephony. In 1944 two more large huts were built, housing a big dance hall and a cafeteria. St Dunstan's went on to buy Brockhurst, a former private school, for £250,000. The 35-acre grounds provided plenty of space for more huts for industrial training and sports activities, along with a swimming pool. In 1943 another property, Belmont, was acquired to house the growing number of female blinded casualties, along with the Essex Hotel, Battlefield, a big house, and the Denehurst Hotel in the local area.

During the war years St Dunstan's largely took over Church Stretton, but the local population showed no resentment. Pauline Haycock remembers that her father acquired a special set of Braille dominoes so that St Dunstaners could play:

"If there were two of our locals wanting a game of dominoes in a foursome they would get two of the blind boys to join them without any trouble. They were all friends together. Pubs were different in those days. Everybody was friendly and talked to one another...the blind boys could tell who people were by their voice. They'd only got to hear you say 'hallo' and they knew who it was.

"They were all special – our home was given to them if they wanted a comfort, to talk about anything. They were all welcome, there were very few that were naughty boys. My mother became quite closely involved. She didn't intend to but she just couldn't help it. She used to take them dancing and into the pictures in Shrewsbury. My impression of it was that people just seemed to want to help.

"Everybody was ready to take them out, see them across the road, to take them dancing, [play] dominoes, darts, take them to Shrewsbury and Ludlow rowing on the river. St Dunstan's and the boys, as they were known, brought life to the town. I think Stretton wouldn't have been such a happy place during the war if they had not been here."

Another Church Stretton resident, Mary Marsden, also remembered the arrival of the St Dunstaners:

"We didn't know what St Dunstan's was. Then hotels were taken over one by one, and the first to arrive was Harry Preedy. As battles wore on the trickle became a flood. They learned to type if they had hands. They learned confidence. They started to live again. That is when the town more or less took over. Everyone was involved. They had people to tea, to whist drives; the girls went to dances; they were the front end of a tandem. Cinemas in the area were filled with a constant buzz beneath the sound track. That was the commentaries by the escorts for their blind companions. No-one minded or hissed at you to keep quiet."

But Mary Marsden tells of another side to the story:

The founder of St Dunstan's
Sir Arthur Pearson Bt., G.B.E.

Fifty years as Chairman:
Lord Fraser of Lonsdale
on the terrace of the
Houses of Parliament.

This dramatic drawing vividly portrays the work and spirit of St Dunstan's. It is based on the legendary Angel of Mons. The signature Craven Hill is that of the artist Leonard Raven-Hill, whose works appeared in *Punch*.

St Dunstan's, Regent's Park: the clock that gave the house and the new organisation their names can be clearly seen.

(Above) Early student masseurs at Regent's Park.

(Below) Individual tuition in the busy Braille Room.

(Above) War-blinded walkers with their sighted guides in a race round Regent's Park.

(Below) Defeated St. Dunstaner penalty-takers make a presentation to Arsenal goalkeeper Ernie Williamson.

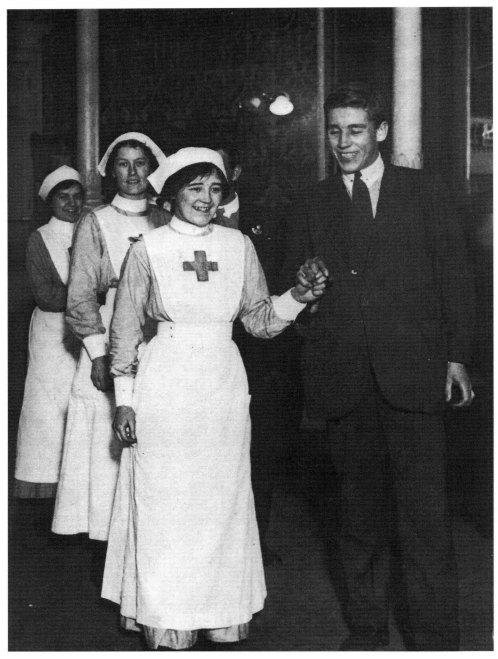

Tommy Milligan, the second blinded soldier to join St Dunstan's in 1915, leading the dance, accompanied by a VAD.

First World War St Dunstaners with their blind teacher, Mr Atkinson, in the Joinery Workshop.

Ian Fraser and Irene Mace (later Fraser) rowing on Regent's Park lake.

The people of Church Stretton welcome returning blinded prisoners of war.
(*Copyright Express & Star*)

St Dunstaners walking 'down the wire' at Church Stretton – (left to right) Harry 'Johnnie' Cope, Brenda Rea, Elsie Aldred and Alan Reynolds.

St Dunstan's singing duo: Beryl Sleigh (left) and Gwen Obern (right), with actress June Sylvaine.

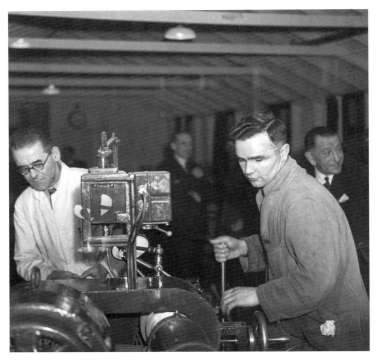

Learning to operate a capstan lathe in the workshop at Church Stretton.

Church Stretton industrial and factory workshop.

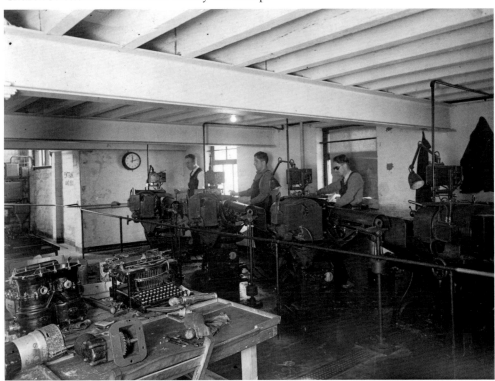

First War St
Dunstaner,
Tommy Rogers
teaches newly
blind actor,
Esmond Knight,
to type.

Mary and John Lawson were the only married couple to come to Church Stretton. They were blinded in an air-raid, along with their daughter Sylvia, who also accompanied them.

(Above) Scenes from the shows performed at St Dunstan's.

(Below) A ward in the eye hospital at Ovingdean.

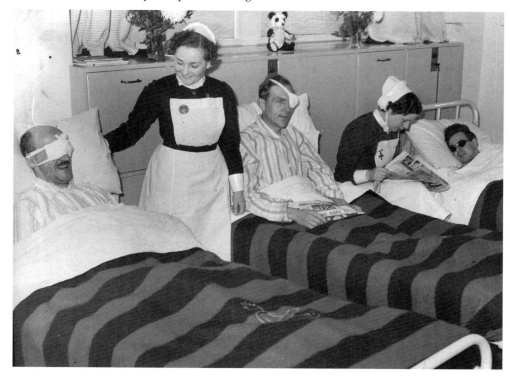

(Above) Dickie Brett prepares to throw using the device that holds and releases his dart.

(Right) Skier Gerry Jones was blinded in a peace-time helicopter crash.

(Below) Archery at Ovingdean: As Norman Perry takes aim the back of his hand holding the bow brushes against the tactile 'sight' that guides him.

(Left) Race walker
Les Dennis ran a
shop when he was
not on the road.

(Right) Alan Wortley is
the physiotherapist
manipulating a patient.
He lost his sight serving
with Royal Navy during
the Malayan emergency.

(Below) Young Ray Hazan, now President of Blind
Veterans UK, using the Kurzweil reading machine.

(Right) Tommy Gaygan, blinded by a booby trap in North Africa, operating his specially adapted switchboard without hands.

(Left) Bill Griffiths, (who was made blind and handless by an explosion while a prisoner of the Japanese), typing in his office.

(Above) Ray Sheriff attacking Crib Goch with a sighted escort behind him.

(Below) Jimmy Wright with his wife Jan and sons Christopher and Nicholas after receiving his OBE.

"It was not all plain sailing. There were many courageous people, and there were many with problems. Mostly they helped each other. Inevitably, there were some who were suicidal. My father and the local Catholic priest, Father Porter, set up a 'bridge watch'. This was the railway bridge – you can hear a train coming. Just very occasionally Dad or Father Porter would catch a young man on the bridge and, in the best psychological jargon of the time, 'ply him with strong drink'. Not knowing where he was, the young St Dunstaner would be guided back to Longmynd Hotel and handed back to his friends. People probably just thought that Mr Wilson and Father Porter were given to drinking heavily!"

Thankfully for the vast majority things were quite different. This is graphically described by St Dunstaner Bob Lloyd, who arrived in November 1943:

"Stretton was one of the happiest years of my life. I look back upon it with much affection. The people and staff were so kind and understanding. When I arrived I was very low, I thought, 'What's left?' The St Dunstaners more or less educated me. 'Come on, you don't want to go yet. You stay here, you'll have a damn good time.' It was a bit of a revelation. It didn't take me long to realise they were enjoying themselves and it's gone on from that day to this."

Yet initially Bob Lloyd had to be persuaded to stay. He arrived in an ambulance unable to walk after 11 months in hospital:

"I had five operations on my eyes but, unfortunately they were not successful. I was to see Mr Davenport, the ophthalmic surgeon to decide whether I was qualified to come to St Dunstan's. This was at Tiger Hall, the hospital wing. I remember sitting waiting. I'd made up my mind I wasn't going to stay. I told myself my family wouldn't want me to stay in an institution. Mr Davenport took the wind out of my sails: "All right, you can go now if you like but looking at the state of you - you can't stand - if I were you I'd wait until tomorrow morning"."

By the morning Bob had changed his mind and this is why: "The late Wally Bowerman, a great Cockney character, cottoned on to me because I could see a little bit, "Can you take us down to the pub tonight?" This was my first night! I said I couldn't walk. 'Don't worry we'll carry you,' was the reply". Armed with late passes from Miss Postlethwaite, the Medical Matron, they set off: "It must have been a funny sight because two crossed their hands and made a kind of chair and I had about half a dozen either side of me all linking arms. I would say, "mark time on the right" and they would swing round the corners in good army fashion". Wally christened Bob 'Hopalong' and, during his first stay, the combination of Bob's remaining vision and his colleague's legs became routine. There were drop off points at each of the pubs in the town, and eventually Bob "would end up at the last pub and I had to wait there until they were ready to come back".

Bob has a fund of stories like this of his happiest year, among them one about a parrot. Pets were not allowed at St Dunstan's but the parrot was admitted when his sailor owner, Danny, refused to stay without him:

"Like a lot of naval parrots he knew one or two choice pieces of language – much to the embarrassment of some of the VADs. In the lounge at the Longmynd, right up in the corner, near the ceiling, was a loudspeaker. One day I took the parrot, climbed up and put him on the loudspeaker. We turned on the radio as loud as we could – the language from that parrot! No VAD could get up to bring it down and the parrot was carrying on like billy-oh up there! Well, we got him down unharmed and that was that."

Bob also recalls dancing with some of the female St Dunstaners at the weekly dances. "How they had faith in us I don't know. It's all right a blind girl dancing with a sighted chap but dancing with another dim must be pretty courageous". Lest it be thought that it was all play and no work for Bob, during this time he also trained as a physiotherapist and went on to establish a prosperous private practice in the years after the war.

* * * * *

Dorothy Pain brought St Dunstan's to Church Stretton as Matron-Commandant, but changes in managerial staff were made during the war years. In the summer of 1941 Mr I.W. Bankes-Williams became Director of

Training, then in 1944 Director of Education. Under Dorothy Pain and I.W. Bankes-Williams were a number of 'First War' St Dunstaners, who came to Church Stretton as instructors. Two of them have already appeared in earlier chapters: Tommy Rogers and George Killingbeck, who were both teaching Braille with Leslie White and Rupert Graves. Joe Walch taught Braille and typewriting, while Sidney Kitson instructed St Dunstaners in boot-making, and Norman McLeod Steel, better known as 'Jock', came to teach physiotherapy on the death of his predecessor, Edmund Toft. Tommy Milligan, with whom we began this history, had also come back to teach Braille. By this time Tommy had also become fluent in German in connection with his employment in business and towards the end of the war he began teaching Braille and typewriting to blinded German prisoners of war in a camp near to Church Stretton. The Chaplain was also a St Dunstaner, Andrew Nugee, the first war-blinded man to be ordained.

In October 1941 Mr Davenport reported 15 cases admitted during the period from all the services, including two Polish servicemen: 'Of these one has been discharged and six have been transferred officially to the training side or have started training in earnest prior to transfer'. At that time 33 St Dunstaners were in training. Twenty-eight were learning Braille and one was learning moon, another form of embossed writing, easier to read by touch but not able to be written. A third were learning typewriting, with four also studying shorthand and telephony; 12 were on the joinery course; seven on basketry; eight on wool rug-making; and two were engaged on a physiotherapy course. Eventually 700 war-blinded men and women would pass through Church Stretton between 1940 and 1946. They included Americans, Estonians, Frenchmen, Netherlanders, Poles and Serbs, as well as those from the Commonwealth countries.

Just as in the First World War, sport played an important part in their rehabilitation. With their own pool at Brockhurst, St Dunstaners had ample opportunities for swimming and events in the pool were part of the programme on Sports Days. Rowing was not so easy. It was limited to one afternoon a week on the Severn at Shrewsbury, where the boys from Shrewsbury School gave up their free time to act as coxes. On Sports Days there were all the usual events: the sprint (incidentally sprint times were much the same as those achieved at Regent's Park); standing long jump; discus; and throwing the cricket ball. The tug-of-war was a team event between houses. One of the innovations was the use of blank ammunition in a .303 rifle as the starting pistol!

Less competitive recreations were tandem cycling, horse riding and hill walking. Tommy Rogers was leader of the Salopian Alpine Club, a group who bravely set out in all sorts of weather. There was a well-equipped gymnasium with punch ball, wall bars, rowing machine and wrestling mat. Other indoor activities included darts and dominoes. There was a flourishing debating society, started by Edmund Toft, while Lady Buckmaster, a volunteer Braille teacher, ran the dramatic society. One of Lady Buckmaster's stars was Esmond Knight and, no wonder – in civilian life he was a successful actor who could have been described as a matinee idol. Esmond had come to prominence playing the lead in a West End production, *Waltzes from Vienna*. His career had been going well, with parts in musicals and straight plays. This was all changed with the war and Esmond joined the Royal Naval Volunteer Reserve. In the pursuit and sinking of the German battleship *Bismarck*, Lieutenant Esmond Knight was on the bridge of the HMS *Prince of Wales* when it was hit by a shell from the *Bismarck*. The ship's captain was killed and Esmond was blinded.

So Esmond came to Church Stretton to study Braille and learn to type. He had already decided that he would return to the theatre and in the meantime joined enthusiastically in the amateur dramatics, both taking part and coaching his colleagues. He also recalls the humour: "Somebody sent us a song saying, 'Dear St Dunstaners, I am sure all you dear boys would like to learn this jolly song I have composed for you. I am sure it will give you great heart when you are walking to work in the morning. It goes Tap, Tap, Tap jolly St Dunstan's boys.' She sent it to us and suggested we all sing it – it soon got a fairly rude version set to it".

Esmond succeeded in his return to stage and screen. His first break was a radio series on the BBC, arranged by Ian Fraser. After that he played Llewellyn in Laurence Olivier's 1944 film *Henry V* and had the strange experience of reliving the incident of his blinding when he played the part of the Captain of the *Prince of Wales* in the film *Sink the Bismarck* (1960).

* * * * *

Esmond Knight would not be the last talented St Dunstaner to tread the boards. St Dunstan's had always recognised the value of music and in the 1930s Henry Hall, whose band played regularly on radio, had become Honorary Music Adviser. In 1943 Ian Fraser wanted to create a music school at Church Stretton under the guidance of a professional Director of

Music. The man Henry Hall recommended was Claude Bampton, who arrived in January 1944 miraculously accompanied by a shipment of musical instruments. Although St Dunstaners had not thought much of the 'Tap, Tap' song Esmond Knight described, they reacted favourably to the music school.

Over the last two years at Church Stretton, Claude Bampton staged 11 full-scale revues, each with a cast of around 50 performers, and 35 concerts. From small beginnings the St Dunstan's dance band grew to big band size, and its players were clad in uniform, red jackets and black trousers, just like the professionals. There were other combinations: the rumba band; accordion band; and, interestingly, a string quartet made up of members of the same family, Jock Steel, his wife, Florence, and their two daughters, Janet and Alison.

Joe Walch's daughter, Joan had come to Church Stretton with her mother in 1942, a year after her father became an instructor. At first she worked in the local Council Offices but later, as she was a good pianist, Joan became Claude Bampton's full-time assistant and a member of the Fol de Rols concert party. Joan met her husband, Bob Osborne, a St Dunstaner who had been blinded and lost an arm and leg, at Church Stretton. Theirs was one of many war-time romances in the town. Joe Walch initially disapproved, according to Bob: "Joe Walch didn't think a lot of his daughter marrying another St Dunstaner". However, the couple proved him wrong and enjoyed a long and happy married life. Bob ran the sales kiosk at Ovingdean for many years, and they carried on the Church Stretton entertainment tradition by forming the Three Blind Mice with St Dunstaners Ron Smith and Winston Holmes.

In the square in Church Stretton, the Orange Tree Cafe was another establishment that was very popular with St Dunstaners. The proprietor, Miss Smallwood, had a young assistant, Sybil Page, who, like so many other young women, was also a volunteer worker and escort for St Dunstan's. In June 1943 a young St Dunstaner walked into the café and another Church Stretton romance began. He was David Bell, a Scotsman with a broad accent, who had served in the Royal Engineers in North Africa until he was blinded and lost both hands clearing a pathway through a minefield. Sybil escorted him on many occasions and their friendship grew. They were married in Shrewsbury, in September 1944. In the meantime David had taken part in training as much as his double disability allowed. He became a member of the dance band, playing trombone using special attachments to his arms.

Their tobacconist business in Edinburgh was successful and David was able to put it in the charge of a manager. He started a course at Edinburgh University and was awarded the degree of Master of Arts. He then went on to earn a Bachelor of Commerce degree – all with the aid of Sybil, who at first attended classes with him and read books aloud for him throughout. In later years, David became the Founder Chairman of Edinburgh Forty-One Club (former Round Table members). He became national president and represented the organisation at international conferences, where his flair for languages helped considerably. He could speak French, German and Russian and understood Dutch, Afrikaans and Spanish – not bad for a blind man.

David's talents led him to be appointed to the Scottish Board of the BBC as well as representative for the disabled on Scottish local and regional hospital boards and the Disabled Advisory committee of the Ministry of Labour. For his public services in Edinburgh, he was awarded the MBE in 1972. David and Sybil had a son, David, and a daughter, Diana, who were both at Buckingham Palace for David's investiture. Theirs was a shared, successful life.

* * * * *

The St Dunstaners who so surprisingly spoke of the early days of their blindness as some of their happiest, always felt a sense of gratitude to the people of Church Stretton. When in August 1946, the time came to return to Ovingdean and Brighton, Ian Fraser made a farewell speech after the last concert: "We will remember Church Stretton with pleasure...and especially we will remember the ordinary people, who made us feel at home, many of whom, in fact or memory, have become our life-long friends".

Pauline Haycock was one of those friends and she found Stretton quiet after the St Dunstaners had left: "You walked down the street and there were no boys there. It took a long time to get adjusted again to the quiet life of Church Stretton. My childhood days were happy. They made them happy. They'd lost so much that they wanted to make up for it".

In 1987 the St Dunstaners returned to Church Stretton in force. Once again the Longmynd and other hotels were taken over, and once more the railway station was thronged with St Dunstaners and their escorts. The occasion was inspired by Mary Marsden and David Bell, who had decided it was high time that some permanent memorial of St Dunstan's war-time presence was established. This took the form of a plaque, carved in wood with the lettering picked out in gold leaf. The inscription reads:

'This tablet was unveiled on October 18th, 1987. It is an expression of gratitude from St Dunstan's to the people of Church Stretton for the warm friendship they gave to war-blinded men and women and their families during the Second World War. From 1940 to 1946 the work of St Dunstan's was centred in this town. Some 700 newly blinded service men and women received their training here and learned to live again in this community.'

The inscription is repeated in Braille on a separate brass plate and both plaques are in the Church of St Laurence.

A dinner in the Longmynd Hotel was the occasion of many reunions of those who had trained together so long ago. With them were guests from the town including, of course, Mary Marsden and Pauline Haycock.

Chapter 16

Bombs on London

'No one has yet missed a day's work',

(Ian Fraser, on St Dunstan's Headquarters staff during the Blitz)

While so much was happening in Church Stretton, there was still a great deal going on in London. The St Dunstan's Executive Committee continued to meet in Regent's Park and several departments remained there, including accounts, welfare, appeals and publicity. The appeals department was under particular pressure at this point, as fundraising was now increasingly important.

The British Legion had agreed to assist in the establishment of a War Fund by allocating ten per cent of the proceeds of the Poppy Appeal to St Dunstan's. Meanwhile the British Empire Cancer Campaign was closing down its appeal and the campaign's staff joined the St Dunstan's appeals team in 1940. In November 1941 their head Ernest Stanford became St Dunstan's Appeals Organiser. Stanford was a redoubtable fundraiser and his work during the war and afterwards into the 1950s was a very important factor in the strong financial position that St Dunstan's enjoyed in the immediate post-war years.

Soon the attentions of the Luftwaffe began to hamper the work of the St Dunstan's staff in London. In September 1940 the first of three high explosive bombs exploded just outside the gate of the headquarters. Within a few days another bomb fell, adding further damage to buildings. On 20 October came the worst incident, the ARP reported two explosions but only one bomb crater at St Dunstan's. Ian Fraser described the bombing in the *St Dunstan's Review*:

'We have had another bit of bad luck. Our offices seem to be a target, though why I cannot imagine, because they have no military

significance whatever. A bomb fell directly on the Talking Book recording rooms...The studios, recording rooms, experimental workshop, proof reading room, were all completely destroyed and in place of a splendid and efficient building there is now a heap of concrete bricks and rubble. In the middle of it all are scattered bits and pieces of microphones, amplifiers, loud speakers and recording machines.'

The whole building was badly damaged by the direct hit, as was the Frasers' own home. The offices were temporarily moved into the adjoining St John's Lodge, which happened to be empty. The staff worked on, despite the lack of windowpanes in the building and were praised by Fraser: 'The greatest credit is due to the whole of the staff for the way in which they are carrying on in these short and difficult days. No one has yet missed a day's work'.

Field staff working outside London were not immune to the bombing either. In September 1940, two of St Dunstan's welfare visitors, Miss Hensley and Miss Morris, were motoring to an appointment when a German aircraft raiding in daylight approached. The two women abandoned their car and ran for shelter in a cottage. They were caught in the blast of an exploding bomb and Miss Morris was severely, but happily not mortally, injured. Through the vagaries of high explosive that became familiar as the war went on, Miss Hensley only received a scratch.

The bombing continued and by the end of the year it was clear that alternative arrangements had to be made. The greater part of the London administration staff would have to be evacuated and, eventually, a temporary base was found at London Colney, in Hertfordshire. But Fraser was determined to keep a London address for appeals and publicity. The answer was to move these departments into his home. The repeated bombing incidents had severely damaged the house, so much so that 'eight or ten of the ceilings came down and the roof began to let in the rain'. The Frasers' furniture was 'soaked and damaged' and the couple were finally forced to give up the house as their residence, moving to a house in north London. While in no condition for living in, the Regent's Park house was still usable. 'A few nails and boards have made it weatherproof for the time being', concluded Fraser. So it became the new St Dunstan's Appeals Office, and it was soon 'full of typewriters and files'.

Aside from appeals, the other departments left in London were the stores and sales at Raglan Street, in Kentish Town. Two staff members were based there to deal with any personal interviews requested by St Dunstaners unable to travel into Hertfordshire. During the war years the sales of home handicrafts boomed. With the shortages of labour and of goods generally St Dunstaners were able to sell their products locally, as well as from Raglan Street, where, despite the air raids, the staff maintained their service. Handicrafts had always previously needed some subsidy, but now St Dunstan's craftsmen were earning a profit. Moreover mat makers and netters could feel they were really helping the war effort by providing camouflage netting and mats for anti-aircraft guns.

Other departments had to move out of London entirely. Pensions, health, massage, poultry farming and welfare matters were transported to Tyttenhanger Park, in London Colney, near St Alban's. This may sound very efficient and convenient, but when St Dunstan's first took over Tyttenhanger Park there was neither mains electricity nor telephone. The mansion belonged to the Earl of Caledon and seems to have been in something of a medieval time warp, including a staff of ancient retainers who came with the property. A St Dunstan's staff memo described the difficulties of managing these inherited servants, who seem to have insisted on preserving the formalities of days gone by: 'The two butlers find problems in serving luncheons and clearing the dirty crockery. It is suggested that we have a buffet system in order that these two old retainers could better deal with this little lunch problem'. It became necessary to engage more staff to help Lord Caledon's people and a couple, Mr and Mrs Bayley, came in January 1941 to occupy the lodge and take on the heavy work in the house.

Another problem was transport. Transfers of staff members living south of London to the departments left at Regent's Park and Raglan Street and vice versa were arranged. For those north Londoners working at Tyttenhanger Park, Askew planned that one of St Dunstan's vans, 'suitably adapted', would pick up staff at Watford and near Barnet. On the Barnet route there were soon complaints. No fewer than 17 passengers travelled in the van, four of them on camp stools. There were only waterproof curtains at the back, as it was not possible to fit doors, due to 'fumes from the engine percolating into the van'. Later small buses were brought into use.

Apart from the house staff, some 40 St Dunstan's employees worked in Tyttenhanger Park, within the secretarial, accounts, welfare, massage, estate, research and poultry departments. They remained there for three years until a move back to Regent's Park was arranged in 1943.

Chapter 17

Prisoners of War

"When we step on to that platform we will hold our heads high and sing at the top of our voices Land of Hope and Glory."
(Lord Normanby, on the planned repatriation
of British POWS in 1941)

One of Pauline Haycock's outstanding memories of Church Stretton during St Dunstan's 'occupation' was a day in October 1943, when the town put out the flags to welcome 27 blinded prisoners of war released by the Germans. The local people turned out to line the streets as their coach drove into the town. Pauline was there with her friends: "We were given a little flag and we marched down the road from school in twos and lined up there waiting for the coach. As it came we shouted and cheered and waved our little flags. The one I remember most was Sid Doy. He was sat against a window with bandages round his face and a trilby hat on and he had obviously lost his nose. I felt very sad about that". It is good to know that at the reunion in 1987 one of the happiest meetings was between Pauline and Sid, when he presented her with a souvenir St Dunstan's brooch.

Ian and Irene Fraser had met the returning prisoners at Liverpool at the end of their long and anxious journey. From the outset St Dunstan's had endeavoured to trace any blinded soldiers who had been taken prisoner, obtaining information through the War Office about individuals. With the aid of the British Red Cross, St Dunstan's was able to send them comforts and equipment. Ian Fraser wrote to the newly identified prisoners explaining what St Dunstan's could do for them when they came home.

Following Pearson's tradition Fraser also sent each blinded POW a Braille watch. Ridged paper to help them write home was also dispatched, along with material for learning Braille. Fraser thought it might be possible to teach them by some sort of correspondence course with the help of sighted prisoners. This proved to be unnecessary through the initiative of one man. The Marquess of Normanby, a lieutenant in the Green Howards regiment, had been seriously wounded and was a prisoner in a camp, Stalag 8B, at Lamsdorf in Germany. With him were three blinded men, among them Jimmy Shepherd. Jimmy had fought in the desperate rearguard action that contributed to the successful evacuation at Dunkirk and was seriously wounded and blinded.

Jimmy Shepherd arrived at Stalag 8B still needing bed care. The British Medical Officer at the camp, Major David Charters, an ophthalmic surgeon, suggested that he could find someone willing to read to him. That reader was Lord Normanby and as a result he was inspired to try to teach Braille to Jimmy and his two blinded colleagues, Doug Parmenter and Fred Wareham. He had found a Braille alphabet in an old French dictionary and, creating examples of the embossed code by pushing matchsticks through pieces of cardboard, he began lessons. By a mixture of bluff, using the Germans' regard for his noble descent, and telling them he was an official of St Dunstan's, he contrived to have most blinded prisoners sent to the camp. There were 28 in the end. Soon Normanby had became an honorary official of St Dunstan's and was in contact with Ian Fraser, who made sure that material and apparatus was sent off to this mini-St Dunstan's.

In 1941 a repatriation of severely wounded prisoners was planned, including those who were blinded. Jimmy Shepherd recalls a bitter disappointment: "We left Germany in a Swiss train bound for the French coast. After a few days waiting at Rouen we were finally put back on the train. Lord Normanby told us that we were not to be repatriated". A disagreement between the Powers had cancelled the plan. The Germans had decided that the exchange should be one for one and there were many more Allied wounded than Germans waiting on the other side of the Channel.

So the prisoners faced machine-gun toting guards and the long journey back. Jimmy remembers that when they arrived: "Lord Normanby urged us not to let ourselves or our country down, 'When we step on to that platform we will hold our heads high and sing at the top of our voices *Land of Hope and Glory.*' This we did, to the astonishment of the Germans waiting at the station. There was pride in the voices of hundreds of badly wounded men as they sang that song – and it was led by Lord Normanby and his St Dunstaners".

In 1942 the St Dunstan's school was moved to Kloster Haina, where it came to its full flourishing. As well as facilitating the delivery of the equipment from England and providing accommodation, the Germans adapted typewriters to English keyboards. They also appointed a blinded German officer to help teach Braille. Known to St Dunstaners as 'Captain Adolf', he had been blinded in the First World War and was a lecturer at the University of Heidelberg. Captain Adolf had his own room in the camp and, able to speak English, he became a friend of the prisoners. Lord Normanby found skilled sighted prisoners too, who could teach such subjects as typing, book keeping, economics and even anatomy. One of them was Ken Mountcastle, who taught Braille and typewriting. Such was Normanby's influence that his quest for suitable volunteer teachers was passed on to other camps. Ken Mountcastle had been taken prisoner in Crete, serving with the King's Royal Rifle Corps. He arrived at Lamsdorf and heard the request for someone with shorthand and typing experience at evening parade. Ken volunteered and found himself travelling across Germany to Kloster Haina.

From Ken Mountcastle we learn something of the place itself. Pre-war, Kloster Haina had been a home for the mentally handicapped. Half the building was given over to the POWs, but the original inmates still occupied the other half. "It was one pretty big building. You might even call it an infirmary here. It was like a hospital. There were big, long corridors and long staircases". Arriving there Ken found that he was to teach not only typing but Braille. "Consequently I had to learn Braille. It was just like learning Pitman's shorthand. One had to learn the basics of the new outline to words and then it was just application. The straightforward basic alphabet was none too difficult. It's when you come to do the other sort of shorthand notes that you have to work hard. The incentive was the thought that you were doing it for a very good purpose".

Taking into account the special circumstances surrounding a school for blinded prisoners, the Germans were prepared to allow walks outside the building – on the understanding that no attempts were made to escape. Ken explains:

"It was pointed out that if anybody had any ambitions in that direction they would be misguided because the benefits to the blind prisoners from the fact that the school existed would all be eradicated. So we were allowed out and the number of guards it took to control us was not very many. There was no doubt that the Tommies considerably outnumbered the German escort. If it was a fine, sunny day we would be able to encourage them and say, 'Let's go for a swim in the lake'."

Other recreational activities out of school hours included games and a nightly 'book at bedtime', when the sighted instructors took turns in a session reading aloud. Captain Adolf often came to listen to the stories.

One of Ken's pupils was Tom Hart, who had been blinded by an exploding hand grenade in Calais – another casualty of the rearguard action before Dunkirk. Before reaching the haven of Lord Normanby's school Tom had endured a roundabout journey through France, Belgium and Poland. A British Medical Officer discovered him, the only blind prisoner in a camp near Poznan, and arranged for his transfer to Kloster Haina. There he was examined by Major Charters, who assessed him as eligible for St Dunstan's and entry to the school.

"Lord Normanby organised it just like a school", Tom recalled. "We had terms, we had holidays. We didn't go anywhere but we had holidays. Through the Swedish Red Cross we received paper, magazines, journals and equipment from St Dunstan's. We had a pukkah school fitted out – Braille books, typewriters, Braille writers. Lord Normanby formulated a curriculum we had to follow. We used to have end of term examinations".

Among the equipment sent out from St Dunstan's via the Red Cross were musical instruments and soon a band was formed. Tom Hart played the clarinet: "After a style. We only did two entertainments a year because Lord Normanby didn't want it to interfere with our studies. We used to have a band practice once a week and then once in six months we used to put on a concert for the whole camp. We were very well received. We put a cabaret on as well as the band".

Tom still has a programme of one of the concerts, entitled 'St Dunstaners on Parade. To be presented in the Dining room, Block 11, on Saturday 10th April, 1943'. The band opened with its signature tune, 'Smile, Darn You, Smile'. There was a mouth organ solo by Tom Wood, a recitation by Sid Doy, a comic song by Jimmy Legge and songs by Bill Young, who had a fine bass voice. Sketches included the 'Fiery Dragon', a nightclub scene in which Tom Hart played a Cossack, dressed in a costume made from Lord Normanby's pyjamas. Tom also danced with a St Dunstaner in drag: "The only trouble was he was the hairiest bloke you have ever seen and he had to shave all over his shoulders and arms. He wore a backless sort of gown that Captain Adolf had brought in from among his wife's dresses".

The first blinded soldiers Tom met with on his journeys around Europe were Dennis Fleisig and Billy Burnett, a lively Geordie. "I have fond memories of Billy in those times. On one occasion in Kloster Haina he was in bed and a German guard came in and started tearing off Billy's blankets shouting 'Raus, Raus!'. Billy bent down, took hold of his boot and chucked it. It hit the German on the side of the head. Billy was brought up before the Commandant and given three days bread and water. The conclusion to that story is that when the German came in next morning he had his tin hat on!"

Billy Burnett got off lightly after his escapade, perhaps because it happened at Kloster Haina. Elsewhere another prisoner was not so lucky – he found himself in front of a firing squad. He survived, but at the cost of his sight. Bill Slade served in the Middle East with the Queen's Royal Regiment before transferring to Layforce. This was an irregular unit, named after its commander, Colonel Laycock. With them Bill was involved in desert raids behind enemy lines. Later they became the 50th Middle East Commandos. He was taken prisoner at the age of 21, in the rearguard action in Crete.

Transported to a prison in Czechoslovakia, Bill was attached to a small Arbeit Commando working on street cleaning and labouring, "I was prepared to do this as a prisoner of war". However, he later found himself expected to work on a railway which he was not prepared to do. "I was taken every morning with about 18 others to a stretch of line that needed constant attention as it was the main line for war material that was manufactured in Czechoslovakia and vital for the desert campaign". With memories of his own part in the desert war fresh in his mind, Bill decided that working on the railway was war work and contrary to the Geneva Convention on acceptable work for prisoners of war.

"I explained to the guard. He raised his rifle to shoot me there and then. 'The others are doing it so why shouldn't you?' He called me a Bolshevik and threatened to report me to the Camp Commandant. He did so. The Camp Commandant warned me that if I did not go to work with the rest of the men I would be shot". The Commandant left Bill to think it over saying that he would return at eight o'clock that evening to learn his decision. Two other prisoners decided to join Bill's protest. They were Norman Cullity and Lawrence Kavanagh and when the Commandant returned, accompanied by two guards, he found all three prisoners obdurate. His wrath was mainly directed at Bill Slade, whom he regarded as the instigator:

"He went berserk and drew his revolver. He said I was a Red Bolshevik and a troublemaker who had already done solitary confinement for escaping. He had been in touch with German High

Command and a firing squad would be sent at six o'clock the following morning. We were to be shot in front of the whole camp as an example.

"Just before it was time to go to work the Camp Commandant and a German Officer came into our hut. He told me that the firing party was here – did I still refuse? My reply was 'Yes'. It was then that he was informed that Kavanagh and Cullity were of the same opinion as myself, he made no comment only ordered all prisoners outside."

The three rebels were last out. Their fellow prisoners had formed up in their usual ranks but they were ordered to stand with their backs to the barbed wire and facing the hut. "I saw the firing squad being assembled under the command of the German Officer. He was giving the order to load rifles… take aim…Fire…"

"I remember quite clearly a thud to my chest and a tearing sensation in my back but I realised the bullet had missed my heart. It seemed to me a considerable time before I sank to the ground, still conscious of what was happening. It was then that the unexpected and merciless act took place, the German Officer, knowing I was still alive, took out his revolver, placed it against my temple and pulled the trigger. There was a shattering blow to my head and the second bullet passed though my head tearing out my left eye and damaging the right. I was still conscious and alive with full knowledge of the damage that had been done to me, especially my eyes."

Bill survived thanks to the attentions of an Australian medical officer, who gave him first aid and then insisted on Bill's treatment in a German Military Hospital. He was repatriated in an exchange of wounded prisoners, and when he became totally blind he was admitted to St Dunstan's for rehabilitation and training. Bill later worked in industry as an inspector of components until poor health brought about his retirement. At St Dunstan's he met his wife, Sally, a care assistant. They were married in 1966. Supported by Ian Fraser, Bill Slade became the only British POW to receive compensation for his wounds during the Second World War, because they were recognised as a Nazi war crime.

Major Charters treated another prisoner for wounds to the eyes, but this man did not join the school. It was not until 1947, when his sight finally failed that he joined St Dunstan's. Michael Ansell was a regular officer who had followed family tradition into the army. He was commissioned into the 5th Royal Inniskilling Dragoon Guards in 1923. In 1939 he became the youngest commanding officer in the British Army, when he took command of the 1st Lothian and Border Yeomanry at the age of 34. During the retreat to Dunkirk, Mike Ansell was leading some of his men towards the coast. At night in bad weather they sought shelter in the loft of a barn.

They received a rude welcome, as he described in his autobiography, *Soldier On*. 'A hail of bullets came through the floor and simultaneously the door of the loft flew open and I took the full blast of a tommy-gun less than ten feet away'. The farmer had heard them enter the barn and assumed they were Germans. A group of English troops were told of their presence and another accident of war took place. In this appalling piece of bad luck Mike Ansell was blinded and lost four fingers of his left hand.

Disguised as a Frenchman he was smuggled out of a prison hospital by two 'glamorous girls' (his description), who were driving for an American ambulance unit under the International Red Cross. They took him to the American Hospital in Paris, where under treatment his sight began, very slightly, to return. Although his presence at the hospital with two colleagues became known when the Germans asked for a list of patients, his treatment continued while he was in the hands of the Germans. He was involved in the abortive prisoner exchange in 1941, after which he came to Lamsdorf. There he was treated by Major Charters for a time before yet another move.

When he finally arrived at Kloster Haina, Mike's sight was sufficient to prevent him joining the school. On walks with Lord Normanby he recalls collecting sheep droppings to use as fertiliser for the garden they created in the compound. 'We soon made some good flower beds with the help of the men, and I doubt if I have ever had better annuals – there were so many of us that every plant could be lovingly protected'. Mike Ansell gave lectures on equestrianism. Before the war he had been an international polo player, show jumper and a successful show-rider for the army.

After repatriation in 1943 he took up both his love of gardening and horsemanship. Although he still had guiding vision, he kept in touch with Ian Fraser who arranged for him to take a course in horticulture at Reading University. After this Mike farmed flowers at his home in Bideford. In December 1944 he was elected Chairman of the British Show Jumping Association. His ideas for the promotion of horse jumping competitions in arenas such as Harringay and Wembley were so successful that the Horse of the Year show became an annual event on television. Olympic success for British horsemen and women followed and Mike Ansell's name became associated with the sport.

When his sight failed in 1947, Mike became a St Dunstaner, although he still continued with his work in the equestrian world. In 1968 he was knighted, in 1977 he became President of St Dunstan's, a position he held until he retired in 1986. He enjoyed a great friendship with Ian Fraser. Although they were veterans of different wars they were both keen fly fishermen and had an annual, friendly, competition for the most catches in a season. Mike Ansell was twice widowed and in his memoirs, he confessed that, despite fame and success, complete happiness eluded him. He died in February 1994, the most famous of St Dunstan's prisoners-of-war.

A quotation from the final paragraph of *Soldier On* inspired the title of this history. In that paragraph the cavalry officer becomes poet:

'As I sit at my desk in this study, with the large Ilex tree outside and the smell of tobacco plants from the conservatory, when work is done I like to let my thoughts dwell on those things of which I am proud: commanding a regiment at an early age, polo with the Hurlingham team in America, representing Great Britain at Show-Jumping, and above all to have overcome blindness. If I were to look out west I would see beyond the lawn a few lights flickering from Bideford, a mile away, like coloured stars on a cold night; the sheep huddled and still; and in the middle of the field that lopped elm which has witnessed so much. A friend tells me I can't see them, but he is wrong, for in my mind I see things well. They blaze sometimes.'

Chapter 18

Survival in the Far East

*'[These men have] suffered most severely, both physically and
emotionally [and] should be treated with the greatest care and thought',*
(R C Davenport, St Dunstan's opthalmologist on FEPOWs, 1946)

In 1942 the British Parliament gave statistics for prisoners of war in the Far East. There were 3,018 from the British Army; 582 from the Royal Navy; and 72 from the Royal Air Force. At first prisoners were mainly taken by the Japanese in Hong Kong, but as the war went on the advance of the Imperial Japanese Army (IJA) caught thousands more.

In September 1945, after the Japanese surrender in August, the IJA offered these figures of those who survived imprisonment: 29,630 British; 11,334 Dutch; 4,662 Australian and New Zealanders; and 296 Americans. These figures were not accurate. Later statistics show that there were in fact, 38,628 British and Commonwealth prisoners released by the Japanese: 32,312 soldiers; 3,388 Royal Air Force men; 1,883 personnel of the Royal Navy; and 1,045 members of the Merchant Navy.

It was time for these men who had suffered so much to return home. In October 1945 St Dunstan's received a warning from the Ministry of Health. It was a copy of a memorandum from the War Office estimating that '300 RAPWI [released prisoners of war] will arrive in the UK with vision of 6/18 or less in the best eye permanently'. It continued, 'of these, about one-half will be unable to do work for which eyesight is essential'. This was a bombshell for St Dunstan's. The initial burden of examining the vision of ex-prisoners of war for potential admission to St Dunstaners fell upon R.C. Davenport, resident ophthalmologist at the charity. Davenport commented that it was not the totally blind that would produce difficulties, but a group of uncertain size who were partially sighted.

Davenport made it his business to examine all candidates as they came home, reporting on each man. By May 1946 he had seen 163 cases. Of these 11 were admitted to St Dunstan's or invited to Church Stretton for discussions about training; two were referred to the Scottish National Institute for the War Blinded; 135 were listed to be followed up at varying intervals according to Davenport's assessment of the prospects of their remaining sight deteriorating further.

Davenport and William Askew, St Dunstan's Business Manager, were anxious that those not qualifying immediately for St Dunstan's should receive adequate resettlement care and pensions. Writing to Davenport, in April 1946, Askew stressed the importance of St Dunstan's keeping in touch with these men, so that if they were felt to be neglected by the Ministry of Labour, St Dunstan's could get involved. 'All these men should get adequate pensions', Askew continued. He resolved to write to the Minister of Labour, suggesting that the Ministry's assessment of cases of defective vision was unfair for those whose vision was impaired but who did not qualify for assistance from St Dunstan's. Davenport prepared a report to support Askew's letter. Among other things he noted that the men he interviewed who had already been considered by the board had pension assessments varying from 40 to 80 per cent. He urged the Ministry of Pensions that as this group of men had 'suffered most severely, both physically and emotionally [they] should be treated with the greatest care and thought, [and] that their pensions should assessed very much individually'.

William Askew was careful to outline St Dunstan's position to the Ministry of Labour: 'We, at St Dunstan's, are taking only a small percentage of these men as the majority are not blind and cannot accordingly be trained as blind people. If we attempt so to train them, we should – I think – be doing a wrong thing psychologically...What these men obviously want is assistance and encouragement'. Referring again to St Dunstan's intention to follow up all cases he concluded: 'we shall probably be left with a residue who are unemployed and unhappy. I then propose to worry the Government in regard to these'.

Askew foresaw the admission to St Dunstan's of many whose vision failed years later. At the time of writing former prisoners of war are still being admitted from time to time. So far 186 St Dunstaner have lost their sight through their sufferings as prisoners of the Japanese. The numbers admitted at the time were much lower than those originally anticipated. As

Davenport had said, the cases of those who were totally blind were straightforward. Some were known of while still in their prison camps.

In January 1945 comprehensive sets of equipment were sent to two airmen: Bill Griffiths and Ossy Gannon. These included materials for studying Braille and for hobbies such as raffia work, netting and basket making. They were sent via the British Red Cross Mission in the United States, in ten metal-bound plywood cases. Each case had a tin container, its lid soldered shut to make it airtight and waterproof. The packs never reached Griffiths or Gannon.

Bill Griffiths caused the most concern. A Leading Aircraftman in the Royal Air Force, he had been taken prisoner in Java in 1942. He was forced by his guards to remove some camouflage netting that they believed was booby trapped. In the resulting explosion Bill was blinded and lost both hands. Sir Edward Dunlop, better known to Far Eastern Prisoners of War (FEPOW) as 'Weary', was then Commander of the improvised Allied General Hospital in Bandoeng. He recalled Bill's arrival there: 'His eyes were shattered in the wreck of his face, his hands blown away, one leg with a severe compound fracture; he was peppered everywhere with embedded fragments, and was exsanguinated [severe loss of blood] and shocked'.

Sir Edward decided to treat Bill, despite the opinion of a nurse that it would be kinder to let him die. Not long after this he had to save Bill from the Japanese, as he describes in his *War Diaries* published in 1987:

'On 17 April 1942 the increasing harshness of the Japanese flared to extreme brutality. Capt. Nakazawa demanded the immediate break-up of the hospital with most of the patients to go to prison along with those medical staff not needed for the few remaining. All were required to move at once. In order to dissuade, I conducted him with his guard to demonstrate the serious illness of many patients. First amongst these was L.A.C. Bill Griffiths...Capt. Nakazawa motioned to the bayonets of his guard. There was a tense moment as I interposed my body before Griffiths and glared at Nakazawa.'

Weary Dunlop's account is typically modest and to the point. Another prisoner who witnessed the incident describes it more dramatically: 'The Japanese guard ...raised his rifle with its stubby fixed bayonet, and putting 'one up the spout' for luck, prepared to lunge. Weary Dunlop placed himself in the way saying, "If you are going to do that, you must go through me first".'

Having survived that, Bill Griffiths lived through three more years of cruelty and neglect, despite his double handicap. In his autobiography *Blind to Misfortune* he recalled his feelings in August 1945 after the surrender of the Japanese:

> *'We didn't feel much different and there weren't many signs of excitement or hilarity amongst any of us. I suppose our resistance was low, and we simply didn't have the emotional energy to respond to the change in our fortunes...I know I wanted to be alone to take it in. I went back to my bed and lay there while my mind tried to focus on the future. Somewhere within me I knew that, during these years as a prisoner, I had been in a sense sheltered from reality. In our fenced-in world I had had round me friends who were basically all in the same boat with me...and were only too willing to help when help was needed. In the wide world outside I knew things would be very different...The truth of it was I was scared stiff and the closer the unknown future loomed, the worse it looked.'*

However, Bill received some small encouragement through a telegram from St Dunstan's. It was sent at the suggestion of Ian Fraser and it read: 'I LOST MY SIGHT AND HANDS WHILE SERVING WITH THE 8TH ARMY IN NORTH AFRICA. HAVING A WONDERFUL TIME AT ST DUNSTAN'S, LEARNING TO TYPE AND PLAY THE TROMBONE, LISTENING TO RADIO ETC. LOTS OF FRIENDS HERE. LOOK FORWARD TO MEETING. (SIGNED) DAVID BELL'.

* * * * *

Bill Griffiths's fellow prisoners also have stories to tell. Their accounts are personal and obtained through interviews and their own writings.

Clarence (Bill) Stalham joined St Dunstan's in 1977, one of those ex-prisoners of war whose sight failed in later years, as forecast by William Askew. Bill Stalham's experiences as a prisoner illustrate the appalling treatment handed out by the Japanese, which has been well-documented elsewhere. Bill was a regular soldier serving with the Manchester Regiment in Singapore when the city fell to the Japanese in 1942. With three other soldiers he attempted to escape. They were captured not far short of their objective, the Burma front:

> *"They literally kicked us all the way back to Changi [the notorious prison camp in Singapore]. We spent three days on the tennis court with our arms tied behind our backs and each time we sagged they would beat us. On the third day they made us dig our graves. They brought my C.O., and the artillery C.O., General Percival, with priests to give us the last rites."* Bill's three companions were shot, *"Perspiration poured out of me. Then General Percival came up to me and said, 'You got away with it – simply because you kept your khaki shorts on.' The others had changed into sarongs. Once they did that they became civilians.*
>
> *"I was one of the first parties, as a prisoner of war, to go up country with 30 men. Our specific job was to clear the jungle enough to put up huts, which were the forerunner of the notorious Burma railway. The hazards were tremendous. We had nothing; no medical supplies, surgical supplies, no drinking water. The main diet came off the coconut trees which we chopped down to make the clearings. Having completed the different camps, we would trek forward through the jungle and put another site up. I think we managed to get twenty of these sites ready for the main party to come up to start to build the railway."*

Bill was taken off this work and sent to Formosa: "We were in small tramp steamers. There were 5,000 of us in one hatch. Each hatch was split into three by wooden divisions. We were placed in these. We could neither sit nor lay. It was terrible under the heat. We were hatched down with one cupful of water per day. The only time we got up in the fresh air was when one of our comrades unfortunately passed away and had to be lowered over the side".

Three days out the prisoners heard sounds of explosions. Allied submarines were attacking the convoy. "Strangely enough we were allowed on deck. We could see ships behind us and in front being sunk. It was amazing, not one of us was scared. Everyone was hoping for a direct hit". Their wish was granted. The ship was struck by a torpedo: "I finished up in the water. I was there for three days and nights, just floating. On the third day a Japanese destroyer picked us up".

Bill arrived in Formosa, where at first he worked with others clearing ground for sugar production. After six months he was transferred to a copper mine: "We thought the work on the reclaiming of the ground was heavy but it was heaven compared to the work in the copper mine. We worked in the nude; no shoes, no tools, only a basket. We were each allocated a hole in the mine and, although there was no substance there, we were supposed to fill three basketsful of copper. If we didn't we were beaten up and our rations stopped. Well, this was impossible". The Japanese introduced mechanical drills and blasting to improve output. "By this method it was still impossible to fill the quota. We would work 12, 14 or even up to 18 hours still not getting our quota".

Bill Stalham was moved yet again. This time he arrived in Japan itself. In his new work he was in his element. A former coal miner, he found himself working in a coal mine on the outskirts of Hiroshima. Here his expertise enabled him to make his work easier:

"Immediately I got to the coal face I would do what we had done in England. We used to hack away the first three inches from the ground for the full length of a stint. The weight of coal above would fall forward without any sweat or hard labour.

"On August 6th, 1945, at 4 o'clock in the morning, the Japanese sentries came round as usual. They used to have two pieces of very hard wood and they knocked them together to tell you the time to come and prepare for work. We went to breakfast, had a small portion of rice, and proceeded to the coal face. We hadn't been working long when everything stopped. There were steel pans with big chains on them that dragged the coal down into tubs. These had stopped working so we could not continue to get the coal out. All this went on for about two hours. The guards didn't want to leave the coal face but eventually we did go to the pit bottom about three miles away from where we were working."

There they learned that all power had gone and that everything had stopped above ground. They returned to the coal face to find the other prisoners and tell them that work was stopped. With the shaft out of action they had to find another way out:

"Fortunately in Japan, as in England, they have to have another safety outlet. We walked up a very steep incline which took us two

and a half hours. When we were nearing the top you could see the Japanese all in confusion, shouting 'Fire bomb!' Some of the people had been on the verge of the blast. I saw a lady with a child on her back and one in her arms. They were all screaming. I got hold of one of the children to help and it just disintegrated.

"Looking up, maybe half a mile away, there was a black wall. It reached the sky and it reached the whole length of the island. We could not believe that just one bomb could cause so much black smoke – it was like a big, black cloud. We later found that this blackness was all particles of dust."

The prisoners' camp had been obliterated and they were moved to another two miles away. Although no work was possible, the guards marched the prisoners each day to the silent mine. Then the second bomb fell upon Nagasaki and the Japanese surrendered. "We still didn't know anything officially until, one morning, an American spotter 'plane came over and dropped pamphlets. They advised us to put something out to indicate the whereabouts of the camp so that they could drop supplies. We used all kinds of materials to make the required signs on the ground. It was heaven for us, when, in the afternoon, a 'plane load of coloured parachutes started coming down. On them were large containers containing American food ("It was out of this world!"). From the leaflets the prisoners learned that the Japanese had surrendered; that they were free and would be going home shortly. "We could still see this black cloud. It was slightly less dense; up in the sky it was a bit thinner. Although our original camp was, shall we say, in the red zone, this one was in the amber. The blast had brought it down".

The freed prisoners were not allowed to move through Hiroshima for six weeks. Then a train came to take them to the city harbour. "When we went through it was unbelievable. There was not a thing standing. There were no craters; the railway was perfect, the roads were perfect. Even when we got to the dockside there was nothing standing at all. What I did see were shadows of people who had been really burnt into the ground and were just silhouettes in the shape of people".

So Bill returned to peace-time life. He re-enlisted in the Royal Artillery in 1949, but the privations he had suffered during the war had taken a toll on his health and he was discharged in 1955. He ran a sub post office until his retirement when his sight failed in 1977. After that he contented himself with gardening, keeping poultry and running a Good Neighbour Club and a group for the hard of hearing.

* * * * *

Like Bill Stalham, Alf Lockhart was caught in Singapore. He was serving with the Royal Army Service Corps. On his way up the proposed line of the Burma-Siam railway Alf was among the prisoners who inhabited some of the camps Bill had helped to establish.

"The journey to the allotted camps was made either on foot or by barge. In this instance the journey was made entirely by barge. By now rumours were circulating about our destination. Already there was talk of our having to build a railway. We left the transit camp at Kanjanburi with mixed feelings and without any rations. We were told we would get a meal at the next stop. We did. Five days later at Tarso. We left Tarso in the barges to make our way up river to Kanu. There was already a working party in residence. They had been there a month and already had some huts built. This was a boon to us as it rained constantly until the start of the dry season in December."

Almost as soon as they arrived prisoners started to go down with malaria and dysentery. The two Medical Officers, Major O'Driscoll and Captain McNally were hopelessly overworked, but they somehow managed to persuade the Japanese to evacuate the worst cases down-river to the base camp, which had by then been established at Tarso.

"We continued working from dawn to dusk, clearing the jungle to make a path for the railway. By now sickness was taking its toll. Men were dying. One or two at first, but gradually and relentlessly the death toll mounted. Under such conditions the role of the doctor became increasingly important. Both Major O'Driscoll and Captain McNally were in perpetual conflict with the Camp Commandant Lieutenant Isuki in their endeavours to obtain more food and medical supplies.

"In January 1943, we were joined at Kanu by a party of Australians. Among their number were two men who became very

highly respected by everyone who was fortunate enough to know them. They were Colonel Dunlop and Major Moon. Both officers were brilliant surgeons and Colonel Dunlop also had the quality of leadership and authority which he exercised whenever possible to improve the lot of prisoners of war.

"It was about February or March 1943 when the Japs discovered that the Kanu workforce was building their section of the railway in the wrong place. Apparently, our section was not in line with the rest of the railway! All the work that had been done during the last three months had been fruitless. This heralded the start of the notorious 'Speedo'. During the ensuing months the Japs made ever increasing demands for more workers. The sick were increasing in numbers, the death rate was mounting and the Japs were getting more vindictive as the work fell behind schedule. With the start of the wet season everything worsened. Men who were ill were taken to work by the Japs, despite all the efforts of the M.O.s. Many collapsed while working and had to be carried back to camp on stretchers. All day long the Japs would be shout 'Speedo, Speedo' and at the same time giving all and sundry a whack with their bamboo metre rods."

Relief came when the railway reached Kanu and the surviving prisoners were sent down-river to rest and hospital camps. At one of these, Tamarkan, Alf met Major Moon again. "He was doing sterling work in the surgical ward. He saved many a man's leg with his skill in healing tropical ulcers". Later, at another camp, Chung-Kai, which was the Base Hospital, Alf was operated on by Colonel Dunlop, who carried out a skin graft for tropical ulcer.

As Commanding Officer, Dunlop set about improving conditions in the hospital as Alf describes:

"Colonel Dunlop first collected all the Royal Army Medical Corps and Royal Auxiliary Army Medical Corps, who were in the camp and put them to work as nursing orderlies. He then decided to get rid of all the vermin from the hospital wards. This he did by organising working parties to disinfect the hospital. Everything that could be boiled was boiled. This got rid of the lice. The next job was the bamboo slats on which we slept. Many fires were built and the slats were passed through the flames until all the bed bugs had been destroyed.

"He organised a diet which suited the needs of patients suffering from various ailments. Where all this extra food came from, I do not know. With Colonel Dunlop in command, it certainly went to the ones most in need. During the next 12 months large parties of men were sent to Japan. We were to learn later that a number of transports carrying these men were sunk by Allied submarines. What a sad thought...to have survived the Railway of Death, only to be drowned and by our own forces at that."

Those prisoners who remained in Siam were engaged on the upkeep of the railway: "Work parties were sent up and down the line wherever the need arose. The biggest problem was the encroaching jungle. We were not greatly troubled by the RAF, except at Non Pladuk, where a large number of men were killed or injured".

When the war ended Alf was in a hospital camp. He did not think much of the first camp orders put up by a British Camp Commandant. These read: 'All British personnel below the rank of Sergeant will parade at 06.30 hours tomorrow for P.T. Only leg amputees are excused from this parade'. "What a profound thought!" Alf concluded. "After more than three years of being worked to the point of exhaustion, all our Officers could do for us was to organise a P.T. parade".

Alf did not join St Dunstan's until 1976, although the organisation had trained him earlier as a 'borderline' case and kept in touch until his sight finally failed. In the interim he had worked as a wood machinist, and as a blind man he turned to hobbies including amateur radio, picture framing and gardening.

* * * * *

Unlike the prisoners from Europe in 1943, the Far East prisoners of war had no ceremonial return. The majority have been victims of slowly deteriorating vision. In many ways this makes acceptance and adjustment to the onset of blindness more difficult. Their training has been individual or as members of only small groups. They have lacked the encouragement of being among a large group of men sharing the same problems. Their treatment by the Japanese has left a long legacy.

All of St Dunstan's ex-prisoners of war are invited to attend an annual reunion at Ovingdean. There was one special occasion when, on 6 October

1987, a group of FEPOWs met at the St Dunstan's Headquarters to greet a special guest. It was Colonel Edward 'Weary' Dunlop. Among the St Dunstaners were men who had known Weary Dunlop personally in the prison camps. Some of them owed their lives to him. To all of them, he was a legend. It is somehow appropriate that in the inevitable group photograph, the Colonel, although at the back, stands taller than everyone else.

Chapter 19

Tembani:
'Home from Home'

'To hope and go on hoping'
(Local translation of the word 'Tembani')

Lord Normanby's school at Kloster Haina was not the only overseas branch of St Dunstan's during the Second World War. Because the Mediterranean area was a battlefield on land and sea, war materials and reinforcements for the Middle East campaign had to make the long journey around the Cape of Good Hope. Casualties also had to be evacuated by that route. Wounded men needed rest stops on their way and South Africa was the obvious place to break the journey.

Early in 1941 an arrangement was made between the British and South African governments that casualties from the Near and Middle East should be sent to military hospitals in South Africa. Casualties would almost certainly include blinded men. The Committee of the St Dunstan's After Care Fund for South African Blinded Soldiers, chaired by Brigadier-General W.E.C. Tanner, arranged with the Imperial Forces for any blinded casualties to be sent to the Military Hospital at Wynberg, Cape Town.

Ellen Chadwick Bates had gone to South Africa in 1930, to take over the organisation of St Dunstan's work in South Africa from the Vintcents, who were retiring. Now she had a new responsibility: setting up a training centre near the Military Hospital in Wynberg. This would provide initial rehabilitation and training, as well as recuperation in a peaceful environment for St Dunstaners before their journey back to Britain and Church Stretton.

TEMBANI: 'HOME FROM HOME'

In September 1941, the Imperial Forces Medical Service was pressing St Dunstan's for reassurance about their capacity to take blinded casualties. There were two already at the Wynberg Hospital and a naval officer in Simonstown. General Tanner ensured that all these men were receiving preliminary training in hospital. In October Norman Kennedy, the proprietor of a building contracting firm, offered the use of his large house, standing in three acres of grounds and situated on the quaintly named Hen and Chicken Hill to St Dunstan's for the duration of the war. Not only was it offered rent-free but also his company undertook to pay all rates, taxes and water charges.

Appropriately, the house was called Tembani – appropriately, because this native Xhosa word means 'To hope and go on hoping'. A building was eventually erected on the tennis court, housing two wards, a small sick ward, a dispensary and four classrooms and workshops. Tembani was opened officially on 18 February 1942, with five new St Dunstaners already in residence. Hester Pease, a St Dunstan's aftercare visitor, had travelled from London to became Tembani's matron, and other staff were appointed, including two First War South African St Dunstaners, Wilfred A. Helm (Braille and baskets) and Jimmy Crawford (massage).

One of the first St Dunstaners to come to Tembani was Max Ash, who had been totally blinded in an accidental explosion of a detonator at Suez. Via hospital ship to Durban and train to Cape Town, he arrived at Wynberg Military Hospital in December 1941. Ellen Chadwick Bates visited him with the time-honoured Braille watch. In January 1942, before the official opening, Max moved into Tembani with a South African St Dunstaner, Jack Vincent.

By August 1942, 12 St Dunstaners were in training and two had been discharged from Tembani. The two 'graduates' were First War South Africans who had been admitted for short courses. Training began in the main house as Max Ash describes:

"We started to learn Braille and typing. They started training quite quickly in the building. It had a big lounge and then just one room between the dining room and Matron's office and that's all they had at the beginning. Jack and I started to learn Braille under Wilfred Helm. When someone new came one of the old boys used to show them around. It was amazing how quickly they all adapted to it. I can't remember anybody who was really down in the dumps there."

Jimmy Ellis echoed that thought. Jimmy had lost his sight, his left hand and the tops of most of the fingers on the right hand in an explosion when he investigated a suspicious object beside the track in an enemy minefield. At Tembani he volunteered to write a monthly series of notes for the *St Dunstan's Review* in Britain. In his first column Jimmy described his arrival at Tembani with Fred Ripley and Joe Daly:

> *'We were introduced all round and although I could not remember all the names, I gathered there was a whole host of people assembled as a welcoming party. Then they showed me around, "Over there you see is the piano," said Norman; "Come and have a look at this beautiful radiogram," said Max, and so they went on. All very well for them but they seemed to have overlooked the fact that I could not see. Alas! The joke was on me; they were all in the same boat as myself. It took me some time to realise this because it was really uncanny the way these chaps dashed about the house. Now it is no longer a mystery. After six short weeks of training in self-confidence and self-reliance, I am now nipping up and down and in and out as if I had lived here all my life.'*

It is clear that the St Dunstan's philosophy of the blind leading the blind had successfully taken root on the other side of the world.

The new building was completed by September 1942. It included two long wards with bathrooms, showers and toilets and a sick bay. As for training, Max Ash remembers: 'The facilities became quite good. There were nice big rooms for basketry, they had a small telephone exchange so that those interested in that could get in some early training. There was a room for the teaching of typing. The typing teacher was a Mrs Spender; of course she was nicknamed 'Sus'. Mrs Lancaster taught Braille and Latin – that was for the masseurs'.

Young South African ladies gave up their spare time to volunteer at Tembani as VADs and were unsparing in their efforts to help St Dunstaners. Yet one lazy and self-obsessed man was deemed to take advantage of them and of his fellow St Dunstaners, who had their own way of lampooning him. A notice appeared on the board over his name:

'ORDERS FOR VADs – DAILY ROUTINE
• Report to my room at 08.30 hours to wash, shave and dress me. She will then carry me across to my breakfast.

• At each mealtime…that is when I am ready…she will feed me and wipe my nose when needed.
• As I am too lazy to work, she will be with me always to read to me and write my very short letters.
• She will keep all other men from the 'phone so that I may have sole use of it by day or night.
• At night when I am ready to go to bed she will carry me back to my room and tuck me in bed.
• At weekends she will pack my case and carry it and me to where I am not invited (but I always invite myself).
Signed: XXXXXX, The only blind man at St Dunstan's.'

It is hard to imagine anyone as bad as this, but no doubt his colleagues made sure someone read the notice to him. The seemingly harsh judgement of his peers would be part of the process of his rehabilitation, by bringing home to him the error of his ways.

Any lively group of young men, blinded or not, will enjoy their jokes and pranks. One VAD, Joan Clement, who encountered St Dunstaners' mischief when she entered the lounge on her first evening survived to tell the tale: "Our uniform was royal blue with a starched white apron with a red cross and a starched veil. I was dressed up with my shoes polished as if I was going on parade when Ronnie Vincent caught hold of me from behind – his arms clasped around me. Norman Perry took my veil and my belt and my shoes and hid them. I was really frightened to death, I thought, well, my first night and now I am going to have the sack".

Joan soon learned to cope with St Dunstaners and came to know one very well. Max Ash had taken a great liking to her: "I used to make a bee-line when she came on duty to make sure I nabbed her. I used to get her to read *The Life of Sir Arthur Pearson,* which was really an excuse". It may have been a strange method of courtship, but Joan married Max in England after his return and her own perilous journey to join him. The ship she was travelling in was bombed and sunk, and so she arrived in Glasgow with only the clothes she was wearing.

Jimmy Ellis also married a South African VAD, Laura Mullins. They, too, were married in England, where Jimmy worked for St Dunstan's Appeals Department. Later he took up the same work for St Dunstan's South Africa. While still at Tembani, Jimmy edited the *Tembani Times,* a publication produced by the St Dunstaners themselves. They cut the stencils, printed it on a hand-duplicating machine and collated the pages, stapling them together.

Like every other St Dunstan's establishment, Tembani had its own band started by Jimmy Ellis, who played the trumpet. Dr William Pickerill, leader of the Cape Town Symphony Orchestra taught others who were interested and the band used to entertain at civilian blind clubs and played for visitors to Tembani on guest nights. Guest nights were a way of thanking the many citizens of Cape Town who generously invited St Dunstaners into their homes or to events and entertainments in the city. The Cohens, who lived next door to Tembani, allowed St Dunstaners the use of their swimming pool, and later, when numbers grew, gave over a wing of their house as extra accommodation for St Dunstaners. Some of the Greek Royal family, who had found refuge in Cape Town, also invited St Dunstaners to their temporary home for dinner and visits to concerts. Princess Eugenie even became a VAD at Tembani and was instantly recognised by St Dunstaners by the sound of her hearty laugh.

Max Ash sums up the cheerful atmosphere, "Tembani was really home from home. There weren't any real restrictions and if anybody invited you out you had only to let Matron know. What I do remember is the amazing hospitality of the people of Cape Town". There was a downside to this. A few St Dunstaners became spoilt and abused this generosity. Matron Hester Pease was concerned and wrote to William Askew suggesting that the rehabilitation of these few men was hindered by the entertainments and distractions in Cape Town and that it would be better if they were sent home as quickly as possible. The Officer Commanding Imperial Troops had asked her for a report on the behaviour of St Dunstaners, reminding her that they were technically still under military discipline. She stood up for her charges, replying that the majority set themselves a high standard and that all round behaviour was excellent. There were, she said, one or two who, 'could not stand up to this life', and these were the ones she would gladly return to England.

By the beginning of 1943 there was pressure for repatriation from St Dunstan's Headquarters in London. With most military action taking place in the Middle East, South Africa was receiving the bulk of new St Dunstaners and Church Stretton had spaces, while Tembani was becoming full. Ian Fraser pressed for the early repatriation of a group of men who had completed their initial training. However, the Army Medical Services predicted that cases would continue to be sent to South African hospitals for some months but in decreasing numbers. It was expected that military successes in the Mediterranean theatre would eventually lead to the opening of the sea route, allowing hospital ships to proceed direct to England rather than around the coasts of Africa.

In 1944, as berths in hospital ships became available the men of Tembani began to return. Parting with some of them was lamented by Hester Pease: 'I feel we could revolutionise our own old ideas with this generation. Look at Norman Perry – and when Max Ash comes to you please just look at him as [if he were a solid], sighted workman of a skilled type. *Who* is going to do all our electrical repairs when he goes I don't know'.

The ending of the war in Europe in May 1945 meant that, sooner or later, Tembani would be closed, and the fall in numbers training there was causing disquiet in the St Dunstan's Committee. After the repatriation of St Dunstaners in 1944, the numbers in training had varied between four and eight, and it was certain that Tembani would not be required in the future for South African St Dunstaners. After VE Day in 1945 the cost of maintaining Tembani could no longer be justified, and it closed on 30 September 1945. Matron Hester Pease returned to England to take up her former post of After-Care Visitor, in which she remained until her retirement in 1953. Her successor turned out to be a former VAD from Tembani, Margaret Cox.

So in September 1945 Hester Pease sailed for England, bringing back with her supplies of linen, blankets, pillows, towels, etc, which were no longer needed in South Africa but precious in England, where rationing and restrictions had created shortages. However, the work of St Dunstan's in South Africa was not at an end. The St Dunstan's Association for South African War-Blinded Veterans was set up. Among the new staff appointed by Ellen Chadwick Bates was a young assistant who soon made her mark through her caring personality. Natalie Opperman devoted her whole career to the welfare of St Dunstaners in South Africa.

She became a Director in 1954 and Chairman of the Board in 1966. On her retirement in 1986 she became President, a position she held until her death in 1988. The Reverend Michael Norman, a St Dunstaner who was blinded in the Second World War, succeeded her. In recent years, St Dunstan's South Africa has widened its activities to include mobility training for blind people generally and it continues to maintain the traditional close links with the parent organisation in the UK.

Chapter 20

Women at St Dunstan's

"Practically every night we used to go to dances somewhere".
(Elsie Aldred, St Dunstaner)

The first female St Dunstaner was Agnes Peters, who suffered severe burn injuries in an explosion at the ordnance factory where she worked during the First World War. Both Agnes's eyes were removed and damage to her left arm badly affected the use of her hand. She did not join St Dunstan's until 1924, when it was decided that workers blinded in munitions factories should qualify for admission. Agnes had already completed her rehabilitation and training at the Royal Normal College for the Blind, in Upper Norwood, South London. However, while she learned netting at Regent's Park, Agnes was also falling in love with another St Dunstaner. Albert Clewlow had been blinded at Arras in 1916 and, like Agnes, he had severe additional injuries. The couple became engaged and were married in December 1926. Sadly the marriage lasted barely 16 months and Agnes moved to Winchester to live with her sister.

Agnes was closely followed into St Dunstan's by a woman who became something of a legend among the women St Dunstaners of the Second World War, to whom she gave encouragement in their early days of blindness. Born at Ruthin, North Wales, Blodwyn Simon was only 19 years old in June 1918 and working in the English Electric Company's Ordnance Works in Coventry when an explosion of hundreds of detonators blinded her. Blodwyn trained at Henshaw's Institution for the Blind in Manchester, and by the time she became known to St Dunstan's she was making fancy baskets and machining stockings back at her home in Ruthin.

In November 1923 Blodwyn's mother wrote to St Dunstan's on behalf of her daughter to request help in obtaining a typewriter. One was sent as a gift and shortly afterwards Blodwyn was admitted. She continued her craftwork through the 1930s in a garden workshop provided by St Dunstan's. There she produced baskets, knitted by machine and by hand, and repaired cane seating for chairs. She also served as Secretary of the North Wales Blind Society.

Blodwyn was a St Dunstaner for 64 years, the last of which she spent as a resident at Brighton. She died in December 1988 and members of her family arranged for a small memorial to be placed in the garden at St Dunstan's, Ovingdean. Just as important are the memories her fellow St Dunstaners have of her. Gwen Obern expressed some of her own appreciation of Blodwyn's example, when she wrote: 'I will always remember and appreciate everything she did to help me and many others to come to terms with our blindness and other disabilities. She was blinded herself in the First World War, yet this in no way impeded her good will and generosity of spirit to those about her in similar condition, who I know have been very grateful for all she did'.

The Second World War involved women to a much greater extent than the First. The creation of the women's branches of the Royal Navy, the British Army and the Royal Air Force meant that the definition 'blinded in the Services' now included women. Those who were called up could opt for service in munitions and so also qualified. Over the years covered by this history, 46 women came to St Dunstan's as a result of service during the Second World War. The majority entered Church Stretton, but some came later as a result of deteriorating vision. Eleven served in the Auxiliary Territorial Service (ATS); two in Women's Royal Naval Service (WRNS); and three were members of the Women's Auxiliary Air Force (WAAF). Seven more were nurses and others served in Civil Defence and types of civilian service recognised for qualification to St Dunstan's, while 14 women became St Dunstaners through explosions in munitions factories.

In October 1942 it was realised that there was likely to be an increasing number of blinded women entering training. This realisation produced what may seem today a rather prudish reaction from the St Dunstan's Research Training and Settlement Committee, based in Regent's Park and at some distance from where the work was going on. The committee recommended that 'a separate establishment for women trainees should be procured near Shrewsbury, so that such trainees might have facilities for housewives' training and, at the same time, be within reach of Massage, telephony and industrial training facilities at Church Stretton'.

They were overruled by the St Dunstan's Council, which considered that 'such a house should be in the vicinity of the present training establishment so that both men and women could not only receive training in the same rooms and from the same teachers but could equally enjoy under one roof such amenities as dances, concerts'. Early in 1943, Belmont, a house in Church Stretton previously used by staff, was converted into a residence for the new women trainees.

Among the women who benefited from this enlightened ruling was Gwen (Gwenllian) Obern, who paid tribute to Blodwyn Simon. Gwen was, herself, in great need of Blodwyn's inspiration and the therapy of the companionship at Church Stretton. She admits that when she went home from hospital, after her own injuries, she would not dress or leave the house. Gwen was opting out. At 22, and not long married, she was totally blind and virtually handless.

Gwen's accident happened on 5 December 1940 and she was conscious through most of it. It was only her third day at the Royal Ordnance Factory in Bridgend and she was late, having missed the special bus from Aberdare:

"So I went on a service one and the driver begged me not to go because there had been a terrific accident the day before. I said I had to go because I had only been there two days and I might get into trouble. I went into the factory and I had to put on this horrible gear. It was a very long white coat and very thick shoes. I think they had wooden soles. Then all our hair was put up under this round cap like a pillbox. I was in training in the department inspecting detonators.

"I can visualise it as plain today as it was all those years ago. This lady had a tray in front of her and there were nine boxes of detonators. She took a box with 500 detonators that she was checking with a gauge. Then she said, 'I am going to do something now that you girls must never, ever do' and she started shaking the tray so that the detonators would fall into the holes in the box. The last thing I remember was a terrific flash."

Gwen was blown off the stool she was sitting on and fell upon the burning detonators and debris. Her face and body were badly burnt. There were 14 women around the table and five of them, including the instructor were, killed. As well as Gwen, another trainee was blinded and went on to become a St Dunstaner: Marian Elias, who was also from Aberdare. Gwen regained consciousness to find herself among the dead and injured: "I must have moved and a voice said, 'This one's alive'. I remember them putting me on a stretcher and it was pouring with rain. I could feel them putting something very wet on my face and then a blanket all over me. I was taken to the factory surgery, where they amputated my right hand there and then. I remember them asking me my name and I said Gwen Davis, my maiden name, so they didn't know who I was".

When Gwen was finally identified, her husband, Ernie, and other family members came to see her. They could see from the extent of her injuries that Gwen was going to be severely disabled if, indeed, she survived. Gwen herself only gradually came to understand. Through questions to different members of the staff she suspected she had lost fingers. Then the time came when pain-killing injections were stopped: "I still had no clothes, my body was too burnt. Then they took my arm out of the big sling and there was nothing on it. I put my lips to it and I thought, hell, there's nothing at the top!"

When she was discharged from hospital Gwen did not realise that she would never see again, yet the injuries she already knew about were enough to cause her to retreat from life. "I went home and I would not dress at all. I was always in my dressing gown. It wasn't pain, I just didn't want to bother". Representatives from St Dunstan's who visited her were sent away, "I said it's very nice of you to come but there's no way I'm going from my home. I'm not going to any place and wear a grey dress and black stockings and no one there to comb my hair".

Gwen's account of traumatic injury and her immediate reaction to all she went through could be repeated by many of her fellow St Dunstaners. So could her account of her arrival at Church Stretton, after the failure of a final operation to save her sight. The only difference is that Gwen is a woman, one among seven women blinded on service with the woman's forces or in munitions factories who were training in Church Stretton at the time. It was another St Dunstaner blinded in a munitions accident who finally persuaded Gwen to go to Church Stretton. "What brought me to St Dunstan's was a letter from Vi Delaney. Vi sent me a letter telling me all about St Dunstan's".

Gwen's husband and her family advised her to at least go and see. Ernie took her and Marian Elias, who also had needed much persuasion to leave home. Neither of them had travelled far from Wales before. "I remember going up to Belmont. The girls were sitting in the lounge. There was Thelma [Meredith], Barbara [Bell], Sadie [Black, later Stokes], Vi, Emily

[McClarnan], Elsie [Aldred], Brenda [Henderson, later Rea] Sir Ian Fraser, as he was then, was in the lounge with the girls. He welcomed us in and he said, 'I hear you sing' and I got up and sang 'Bless this House'. "

At Church Stretton Gwen finally had confirmation that she was totally blind. The shock added to her homesickness and it was some time before she felt the tonic effect of the presence of the other St Dunstaners around her. As so many others do, she remembers the sense of humour which could only have been shared by those with similar disabilities. "I went to this dance. I was sitting in a corner. Somebody came up to me. It was David Bell, he said, 'How are you?' and I was shaking his hand, his artificial hand, when he walked away leaving his hand in mine. I nearly went though the chair". It was Gwen's first experience of St Dunstaners' jokes and it began her recovery of her real self – ebullient, ready for fun and enjoyment of life. She joined the concert parties and, unable through her injuries to undertake normal training, began the singing lessons that led to her semi-professional career in later life. Gwen has become a prominent citizen in her part of Wales through her singing and appearances on television and radio. Later she became a Freeman of the City of London.

On many occasions Gwen sang in concerts with another St Dunstaner, Beryl Sleigh. Beryl had studied singing at the Royal College of Music and had begun her career in London just before the war. In May 1940 she joined the First Aid Nursing Yeomanry (FANY) and was serving at Aldershot when she was drafted to the 1st London Motor Company, ATS, as a driver. Beryl was in quarters in London when a landmine fell opposite her billet. The windows were blown in and fragments of glass injured her face and eyes, blinding her.

At Church Stretton Beryl's friendship with Gwen began as they both played their parts in the concerts and entertainments. Later their partnership continued as they sang in concerts in many parts of the country, often fundraising for St Dunstan's. Although neither lady managed a fully professional career both kept up their music as a hobby and sang together on St Dunstan's special occasions, notably the reunions organised regularly for the lady St Dunstaners.

Flying glass brought another member of the ATS to St Dunstan's. Barbara Bell was a sergeant serving in a mixed anti-aircraft battery. In December 1942 she was in a train that was attacked from the air:

"I was going on a course on the height finder for anti-aircraft guns when the one-track little train was bombed outside Guildford at a

place called Bramley [in Surrey]. Unfortunately we didn't know there was an alert in progress and when I heard this rattling on the roof I promptly had a look out to see why it was hailing out of a blue sky. Of course, it was machine gun fire really and then he dropped a stick of bombs across the train. That was it – facing the window. If we had known, I would have been on the floor and perfectly OK."

Like Beryl Sleigh, the fragments of glass so damaged both Barbara's eyes that she was blinded. At Church Stretton Barbara soon made up her mind that her future occupation should be physiotherapy. This meant leaving Church Stretton after initial training, to study in London at the Royal National Institute for the Blind's Physiotherapy School. She stayed at the St Dunstan's hostel, joining Mary Wright, whose sight had failed through haemorrhage attacks while she was serving with the WRNS. After qualifying, Mary happily regained some sight and left St Dunstan's but she and Barbara maintained their friendship.

When she qualified Barbara practised in Ilkley, West Yorkshire. She walked to work, a brisk ten minutes from her home, with her guide dog, and after the death of her mother, Barbara lived alone – and she still did at the time of writing. A music lover, she also enjoys country walking with friends, and has climbed Great Gable and Scafell among other hills in the Lake District.

*   *   *   *   *

The youngest girl, indeed the youngest person, to come to Church Stretton was only five years old. She was Sylvia Lawson. Of Sylvia and her family Ian Fraser wrote, 'To me nothing could equal the tragedy of the Lawsons... I had never seen such human misery'. In September 1940 the Luftwaffe attacked the British Aluminium rolling mills in Warrington. Bombs intended for that target were instead dropped on the neighbouring Thames Board Mills, where a tea party and social was taking place. Sixty-three people were killed and 43 injured. John Lawson, a member of the Home Guard and an employee of Thames Board Mills, had taken his wife, Mary and their daughters, Sylvia and Anne, aged 18 months, to the party. Anne was killed; John, Mary and Sylvia were blinded.

All three came to Church Stretton. John came because, as a member of the Home Guard, he was qualified to become a St Dunstaner, Mary and

Sylvia accompanied him because it would have been cruel to separate this shocked family. John went through the normal training. He became a telephonist and went back to Warrington with Mary to work once more for Thames Board Mills. Mary had trained with other lady St Dunstaners, concentrating on cookery and other domestic skills. After Sylvia escaped another bombing at the Sunshine Home for Blind Children in Southport, her parents sent her to live with her grandmother. Ian Fraser arranged a place for her at Chorley Wood College and, after training at Henshaw's Institution for the Blind in Manchester, she became a telephonist like her father. Sylvia recovered some sight after a series of operations. She later married and had two children.

Also in Warrington, later in November 1942 Elsie Aldred received her call-up papers. Her father and brother were already away serving with the forces, so 21-year-old Elsie opted for munitions work to enable her to remain near her mother. It was the choice of a dutiful daughter, but it was a disastrous choice. Yet another detonator explosion in a munitions factory, the Royal Ordnance Factory at Risley, blinded her and severely damaged her right hand. "I was fortunate that, after hospital, I came to St Dunstan's straight away. It was so easy for people to slip through the net in those days, particularly working in munitions".

At Church Stretton, Elsie found herself among eight other girls in training. She chose telephony as a career: "We had to learn reading and writing in Braille. Then I did Braille shorthand and, although I could type before, I had to have a refresher on typing. It is surprising how you forget and I had to learn to do it one-handed". Off duty Elsie and her friends were equally busy, "Practically every night we used to go to dances somewhere. There were a lot of army and RAF camps around Church Stretton and they used to invite parties of St Dunstaners". Elsie kept up her dancing when she returned to Warrington where, despite her blindness, she spent many years looking after her elderly parents. In her sighted days she had worked in the accounts department of a Warrington firm, Peter Stubbs Ltd, and they asked her to return as their telephonist. She retired in 1979 and continued to live alone cooking for herself and keeping house.

Eileen Williams was another telephonist, although she gave up her work with the Ministry of Labour in 1950 when she married. Eileen's sight failed while she was serving in the ATS. Her husband died in 1959, leaving her to care for her eight-year-old son Terry. With the support of her family Eileen brought Terry up and he is now a teacher. Eileen has had the honour of presenting bouquets to two Queens during royal visits to St Dunstan's, to the former Queen Mother in 1948, and to Queen Elizabeth in 1965.

One lady St Dunstaner served in both wars. Maureen Lees lost her sight through her service with the ATS, as Sergeant Major in a Mixed Heavy AA Battery. In 1917 she volunteered to join the Women's Auxiliary Army Corps (WAAC) and became the youngest girl in the British Army. During the celebrations of the Armistice in 1918, Maureen marched in the Peace Parade. During 1944 her sight began to fail and she came to St Dunstan's in June 1945 and trained as a weaver. Back at her home in Birkenhead she established a workshop in an old coach house, operating five looms and soon became well-known locally for her work.

As befits an ex-Sergeant Major, Maureen was a woman of great determination and energy. She organised craft exhibitions annually for the benefit of St Dunstan's funds. Although an expert weaver, her typewriting would cause some headaches at St Dunstan's Headquarters. Lacking someone sighted to check her letters, she was liable to allow her fingers to stray on to the wrong line of the keyboard.

* * * * *

Zofia Bregula's experience of war began when she was a 19-year-old drama student in Warsaw. Working with other young women for the Red Cross, she was fortunate to survive the devastating German air attacks on the capital unscathed. During the occupation the Germans forbade any higher education for the Polish population. All forms of Polish arts – music, literature and theatre – were banned. An underground education system developed, with students being taught secretly in the homes of their professors. Polish musicians, actors and actresses, Zofia among them, gave concerts and recitals in secret venues behind closed doors and drawn curtains.

Zofia graduated in 1944, but she remained in Warsaw and was part of the underground movement. In August of that year the Russian forces were nearing Warsaw and the Polish resistance was urged from London and by the Russians to begin an uprising in the city, which was still occupied by the Germans. It was expected that within a week the Russians would cross the River Vistula and relieve the fighters. They did not come. Abandoned by the Russians, the young Polish patriots were besieged in Warsaw. Zofia was acting as a runner between positions: "We had many wounded boys. Two of them were badly wounded so we were taking them to hospital". This was located in cellars beneath a bank. "I went there and for two days I was bringing water. It was difficult with all the pipes destroyed. I was running and all the street was burning. I went every other day to the other building we were defending to bring them something to eat".

Zofia was in the cellar hospital when it was hit by German shells: "I heard such a terrible noise. When I awoke I was lying on the floor and my first thought was 'my eyes, my eyes'. I wanted to get up but I couldn't". All the Polish wounded, including women and girls, were taken prisoner by the Germans. "They took me on a stretcher. They were gathering the wounded in one place and they put us in cattle trucks". The women prisoners were finally placed in a camp called Oberlagen, near the Dutch border. The treatment Zofia received during this time failed to save her sight. When the camp was liberated, appropriately by Polish soldiers, she and other wounded women were brought to hospital in Edinburgh. While she was undergoing treatment for her eyes and other injuries Zofia met the man who would become her husband; a young Polish violinist named Wlodek. The surgeons restored some partial vision. Thinking that she was not completely blind, Zofia at first refused the offer of training at St Dunstan's.

On Wlodek's advice she accepted a second offer and in September 1946 she joined the St Dunstaners who had only recently returned to Ovingdean from Church Stretton. "There", said Zofia, "I learned to be independent as much as it was possible in my situation and the belief in my future life. Many tasks we all had in St Dunstan's. It was the best way to forget about my worries". At Ovingdean she met Esmond Knight who, although he had been blinded in the naval action with the *Bismarck,* had managed a successful return to his pre-war career as an actor. He and the St Dunstan's authorities encouraged her to continue her studies at the Royal Academy of Dramatic Art. She and Wlodek had kept in touch and he had visited her at Ovingdean. He decided to go home to Poland and Zofia decided to follow him as soon as possible.

"Esmond came to Ovingdean and we had a long, serious and absolutely honest talk about my future in the theatre in England". Esmond's advice that, as a nearly blind actress with a foreign accent she would face difficulties without a patron, confirmed her decision to return to her homeland. She lives in Katowice and over the years she has had a successful career in the theatre and in broadcasting. Sadly she was widowed in 1986. She has returned to St Dunstan's on several occasions to meet up with her friends at Ladies' Reunions.

Zofia sailed for Poland on the *Eastern Princess* with Polish war veterans who were being repatriated. They left with the sounds of a military band playing the Polish and British national anthems and the farewells of friends who came to see them leave. Although the Communist Party did not come to power in Poland until 1947 there were problems in their own country for the members of the Polish forces who had escaped the Germans much earlier to continue to fight for the Allies during the war. In 1945 St Dunstan's decided unilaterally that blinded Polish servicemen should be treated as if they were British subjects. Later this position was regularised as the council agreed with the proposal that, provided that the British Government allowed them stay in this country, eligible Polish and other Allied nationals should be given suitable training. They would be helped in settlement in work and provided with technical after-care. Many stayed on to live their lives here.

For those who wished to return to Poland, St Dunstan's assisted in paying for their repatriation. Those who did faced a mixed welcome. Zofia encountered difficulties in her profession when the Communist government became aware of her part in the Polish underground and the Warsaw Uprising. When the *Eastern Princess* entered the port of Gdynia in November 1947, Zofia and her fellow Polish fighters received a very different welcome from the send off in Glasgow: "Nobody, no orchestra welcomed us in Poland".

Chapter 21

Working in a Sighted World

"Ever since the days of Agincourt people have had short memories of the war-disabled when the fighting is over."
(Lady Apsley, Chairman of the British Legion
Women's Section, 1944)

By 1961 employment opportunities for blind people were almost boundless. The charity proudly recorded that St Dunstaners were working as: 'college tutors and school masters'; 'aldermen and councillors'; 'chairmen, executives, administrators, welfare officers and home teachers of the blind'; 'ministers of religion and lay preachers'; 'solicitors, chartered accountants, insurance brokers, physiotherapists, short-hand typists, telephonists, authors, journalists, public relations officers, labour and welfare officers, a catering supervisor and storekeeper, the director of a printing business, production manager of a film company, garage manager, numerous shopkeepers, a one-armed lift operator, a handless guide at Warwick Castle, piano tuners, a dark room assistant, guest house proprietors, the manager of a fishing and motor boat business, the manager of a market stall, wholesale fish merchants, an antique dealer, a stoker and even a gravedigger'.

This long list of careers could have included another St Dunstaner who was a member of a Yorkshire family of showmen. He toured fairgrounds in a trailer lorry driven by his wife and later owned a sea-side amusement arcade. Also, by this time, specialist engineering jobs in industry were also filled by St Dunstaners all over the country.

Perhaps more surprising than all the occupations carried out by St Dunstaners, must be that of film producer, yet this was the career successfully followed by Jimmy Wright. As a small boy Jimmy went to the cinema more often than he did his homework, "I suppose I should have been spending my time more profitably but I think as I did go into the film industry it has been a tremendous advantage. I started as dogsbody at Technicolour in 1940". By the time he was old enough for the Services he was an assistant cameraman. Following his father, Jimmy joined the Royal Air Force as a cameraman with the RAF Film Unit.

Jimmy was awarded the DFC for his service. He was flying on the 8th Army front in Italy when his aircraft crashed and he was badly burned. He entered St Dunstan's in 1945 and, after years of treatment by plastic surgeon Sir Archibald McIndoe, joined with RAF colleagues in founding Anglo Scottish pictures in 1951. "I was very apprehensive about how useful I could be because film making is a 90 per cent visual occupation". Jimmy persevered to master the many facets of film making, "I wasn't seeing the results of all the efforts but if someone says afterwards that was a very good film then I feel I've achieved something".

Through two companies Film City Productions, making advertising films and Cinexsa Films on documentaries Jimmy has been part of award-winning productions including a Bafta documentary award. He made two successful films for St Dunstan's. A quietly spoken, smiling man he hid a hard core of resolution that enabled him to succeed. For most of his productions he had to raise funds from sponsors, recruit his crews, plan locations, arrange film editing and dubbing sound tracks. In the dubbing studio Jimmy's keen ear was an enormous asset. In his office his main tools were two telephones and a Braille shorthand machine by each. "I find that the shorthand machine is positive, once you have taken a note there it is on paper. You can tear it out and stuff it in your pocket, whereas with a tape recorder I'm not sure if it is working or not".

Using his fundraising skills Jimmy worked for a number of charities. His most outstanding feat was crossing the Channel suspended in a parachute harness above the sea and towed by a boat from which he parascended in aid of the RAF Benevolent Fund. Jimmy married in 1967 and his wife, Jan, and their two boys were at Buckingham Palace when he received the OBE for his charitable work.

Two things had opened the way to the opportunities enjoyed by Jimmy Wright and his fellow St Dunstaners: the shortage of labour in the Second

World War and the Disabled Persons Act of 1944. The act required any employer of more than 20 workers to engage a quota of workers who were disabled.

During the passage of the bill through the House of Commons, Ian Fraser had endeavoured to introduce a preference for disabled ex-servicemen and women. At first, Ernest Bevin, the Minister of Labour, refused to have this written into the bill. At committee stage, more pressure was put on Bevin, who finally agreed to put the preference into the Bill. A comment made by Lady Apsley, then Chairman of the British Legion Women's Section, may have swayed him. She exclaimed that, "Ever since the days of Agincourt people have had short memories of the war-disabled when the fighting is over".

The Reinstatement in Civil Employment Act, another piece of legislation passed during 1944, backed up the Disabled Persons Act, although it affected all ex-service people, disabled or not. Meanwhile, in the House of Commons Ian Fraser urged greater emphasis on the needs of those men and women returning from long periods of service to their country. In a speech to the House in April 1945, he said:

"The signs are that the organised war with Germany will soon be over. We have got to beat thousands of swords into ploughshares and in the process we have got to absorb into our economic life five and a half million men and women who have been out of it for years... Except where the Reinstatement of Employment Act positively requires – and rightly requires – that a man should give up his job to an ex-service man who left the same job to go and fight, the trades unionists and others cannot, and in my view should not, be asked to go into unemployment to make jobs for returning men and women. But wherever vacancies occur there should be a priority for those who have been away."

A year later George Isaacs, Minister of Labour, reported in the House that the Disabled Persons Act was working smoothly. In York, one St Dunstaner had already returned to his old job. Herbert Scaife had worked as a baker before he was blinded in Italy 1944 and was at that time the first St Dunstaner to return to this type of work. Despite successes like this, Fraser was still pressing the case for the ex-service disabled in parliament: "Let me emphasise that more than 2,000 disabled men are waiting for jobs. We understood the disabled were to have a preference in this matter and I would like to know what has happened. At the moment there are jobs, but the men we want to see in them are not in them. How can we get them into them? We can only do so by putting them at the head of the queue". Here Fraser was probably speaking for a wider area of disability than blindness for the prospects for the majority of St Dunstan's trainees were good.

Efforts to find employment for blind people within industry in this country had begun long before this. There were excellent examples in America, where the Ford Motor Company began employing blind men on the factory floor soon after the First World War. In typical fashion Henry Ford had decreed, 'If one out of every thousand persons is deaf then one out of every thousand Ford workers must be a deaf man. If one out of every six thousand is blind then one out of every six thousand Ford workers should be blind'. His edict was obeyed. Each handicapped person received full pay for a full day's work and, where necessary, the company was prepared to adapt machinery so that a disabled operator could work it.

In Germany, as Ian Fraser had discovered on his visit in 1922, blinded ex-servicemen had been employed in munitions factories as early as 1918. A German law passed years before anything similar in Britain, compelled large firms to employ a percentage of disabled ex-servicemen. As a result blind people in Germany were employed in a wide variety of factories. The occupations and conditions of those working for Siemens Electrical Works in a special factory had greatly impressed Fraser, although he doubted, rightly, the long term economic viability of the project.

However, it was not until 1935 that St Dunstan's established a machinery department, where St Dunstaners were taught to operate router and borer machines, a circular saw and a vertical belt sander. The National Institute for the Blind had already long been investigating the possibilities of industrial employment of blind people and throughout the 1930s worked in co-operation with the National Institute of Industrial Psychology. All this went a long way towards proving that blind people could operate machines safely and work in industry. The problem was that, between the wars, industry was not willing to offer them work, nor was thinking in blind organisations necessarily positive. Many workers for the blind believed that the trades normally followed in sheltered workshops were the best solution to problems of employment. Most telling of all was the fact that there were not enough job vacancies for sighted workers at a time of widespread unemployment. The coming of the Second World War changed all that.

With men called up for war service and factories geared for production of war materials, often working day and night, industry was hungry for labour. The first source was, of course, women but now opportunities for blind workers also opened up. The work that had been going on between the wars was to be rewarded. Both St Dunstan's and the NIB were ready to train and supply blind workers for open industry. In 1940 St Dunstan's set up a Research Advisory Committee to investigate potential occupations in industry for St Dunstaners. Several leaders of industry were among its members: the Hon J. J. Astor, then proprietor of *The Times* newspaper; Lord McGowan of Imperial Chemical Industries; Lord Nuffield represented the engineering industry; Sir William Jameson was a member of the Medical Research Council and later Chief Medical Officer of the Ministry of Health. This influential committee was able to open doors to blind workers in different industries and many occupations that, before the war, would have been considered impossible for the blind.

Due to the efforts of the committee a pilot scheme was launched. The type of work on offer to blinded workers was carefully studied and the best possible candidates were chosen. The key criteria were fitness and character. It would not help if these blind workers proved to be unreliable through sickness and they had to be congenial and sociable people who would fit into factory life. The importance of a project that could hold out much wider prospects of employment for the young men in or entering training at Church Stretton could not be exaggerated. In November 1941, Harry Bennett, who became responsible for St Dunstaners settled as telephone operators, shopkeepers, boot repairers and factory workers, summed it up: 'In placing men in jobs we shall continue to select work which is suitable for men (as against women) and preferably work which will provide opportunities for gaining increased skill and also jobs which may themselves extend to the post-war period'.

The first St Dunstaners placed in industrial work were, in fact, First War men. It was decided to invite craft workers to take part. Those in their early forties were thought to be the best candidates and the first of these was Bill Chamberlain. Bill Chamberlain was born in Hull and left school at the age of 14. For three years he worked in a saw mill and then he turned to work on tug boats. Bill became a crew member on a number of Hull tugs, including a sea-going vessel, the *Tyke*, before he enlisted in the East Yorkshire Regiment, aged 21. He was wounded by a sniper in the Ypres Salient in 1916.

After training at Regent's Park, Bill opted for poultry farming, but later he returned to St Dunstan's to retrain as a joiner. He continued in this work right through to the Second World War, and in the interim he met and married Jessie, the sister of another St Dunstaner, Benny Hamilton. Bill recalled how Jessie played an important part in his acceptance of St Dunstan's suggestion that he give up his workshop and take up a job in industry:

"I said, 'No'. I was scared stiff. I think I was more afraid of that than I ever was in the trenches. Yet I don't know what I was afraid of. I tried all the excuses I could use but Jessie and St Dunstan's knew all the answers. After being bombed in the Hull Blitz, we deposited our home in different parts of Derbyshire and got the train for London. Jessie said to me on the train, I believe she knew I was afraid, 'You can't turn back now.' The train had started. I said, 'I don't want to.' That fear left me just like that."

Bill went through another retraining course and went to work for Miles Aircraft in Woodley, near Reading, as an inspector. "It dawned on me – Why am I here? War effort, yes but wars come to an end. Why has St Dunstan's asked me to come? Then I thought of the new men who would be blinded and I thought St Dunstan's want to put the newly blinded men in industry and I am here as an experiment. I realised, 'I've got to do this job right; I can't slip up anywhere'." Bill found that the attitudes of the sighted workers towards their new, blind colleague varied, "According to their intelligence. Fortunately I got in with a decent crowd of chaps. They were willing to help. I showed them I was willing to learn and I could do it if I learned. I found I started to put the specifications on the drawings into Braille".

Bill worked on for Miles Aircraft, and after the war for the company's later incarnation as Miles Martin Pens, when the factory turned to the manufacture of the newly invented Biro pens. He retired in 1950, but in his garden workshop he continued making scale models of steam engines and a four-foot six long model of a sea-going tug. His experiences would have been largely the same as those of his fellow First World War pioneers. Their readiness to take up a challenge in a totally different environment paved the way for their younger colleagues. Not surprisingly, one of them followed Bill Chamberlain into Miles Aircraft. Richard Dufton, a regular in the Royal Navy, had been blinded in an air raid while on an engineering course in

Plymouth. In 1942 Richard began working in the Miles Aircraft Experimental Department on design work for aircraft and engines. He used a tactile drawing board and his own phenomenal memory for facts and figures.

In 1943 Lazlo Biro patented his invention of the ball point pen. Initially looking at the advantages for use in aviation of a pen that could write in all kinds of conditions, Miles Aircraft bought the development and manufacturing rights. The early biro pens were expensive and used a complicated tubular metal ink container. This was doubled back twice on itself to achieve sufficient ink storage and prevent too much ink flowing past the tiny ball at the tip. As Chief Designer, Richard Dufton headed a research project to solve the problems of ink flow. Success in this area led to the development of a straight, plastic tube to contain the ink and created the cheap, universal ball pen that is now used every day. His thesis on *The Technology of Ball Point Pens*, completed in 1960, gained him membership of the Institute of Mechanical Engineers. A year later he became Director of Research at St Dunstan's.

* * * * *

In November 1942 St Dunstan's built two huts at Church Stretton for industrial training. The machine shop was also equipped to provide training on lathes, presses, routers and upholstery equipment. These machines were added to or updated to keep pace with developments in industry. For example, in September 1945 a newly-installed plastic moulding press was successfully demonstrated by trainee Joe Carney. He fulfilled a contract for 4,800 bakelite switch covers as quickly as a sighted person. At that time three more advanced type capstan lathes were introduced. This ensured that St Dunstaners taking up employment were familiar with most of the machines they might encounter in factories.

Soon a steady stream of men were leaving training and entering all kinds of employment. A list of placements recorded the names of St Dunstaners, the type of work they were undertaking and the firms that were employing them. As the list grew it became a regular feature in the *St Dunstan's Review.* By the end of 1949, 260 St Dunstaners were in industrial employment, 144 were telephonists, 53 were running their own small businesses, and 70 were running businesses under a controlled shop scheme. These St Dunstaners were financed and set up in business by the charity and from the profits they paid off the finance until they became the owners in their own right.

The man reporting on all this was himself a St Dunstaner. G. P. 'Pat' Owens began his army service before the war, as a boy soldier, and rose to the rank of Sergeant in the Royal Engineers. When he completed his seven-year term of service he joined the Kent Police Force. In 1939 Pat was recalled to the army and after a period of training Sappers he was commissioned. Pat became Second in Command of 262 Field Company, Royal Engineers. He was three times Mentioned in Despatches and the French authorities awarded him the Croix de Guerre for his bravery in clearing the beaches of mines on D-Day. He served through the campaigns in Europe until, in 1945, he was severely injured and blinded by a mine. Pat endured a long period in hospital before he could go to St Dunstan's for training and afterwards he stayed with St Dunstan's as Industrial Director, starting in 1947. He filled this position for nearly 30 years and made an enormous contribution to the lives of some hundreds of war-blinded men and women.

Pat Owens was not the first St Dunstaner to take over a department at the charity's headquarters. Another Sapper preceded him. Peter Matthews was a Chartered Surveyor in civilian life and had established his own practice in his home town of Plymouth. He joined the Territorial Army and was embodied into the Regular Army in 1939. He was posted to the Royal Army Service Corps in France and went through the evacuation of Dunkirk. Commissioned in the Royal Engineers in 1941, he volunteered for bomb disposal, and three years later he was blinded by one of our own mines planted on a beach at Penzance. Like Pat Owens he had a spell in hospital before arriving at Church Stretton.

Peter Matthews had been made a Fellow of the Royal Institute of Chartered Surveyors in the same year that he was blinded. In 1945 St Dunstan's recognised him as an ideal candidate to take over the task of finding homes for St Dunstaners as Settlement Officer. Housing was playing an increasingly important part in placing St Dunstaners in employment, as it was often necessary to find a home where there was an appropriate job available for an individual. Peter Matthews would give 32 years of his life to the important task of locating and purchasing homes for St Dunstaners. Within Peter's first two years 479 St Dunstaners were receiving housing assistance. The aim was to obtain a house for every St Dunstaner in serious need, which was defined as the need for accommodation near his or her place of work or the desire to move for health reasons or other urgent causes.

There were difficulties in renting houses, so money had to found for more purchases. However, the ideal of providing free housing for all St Dunstaners could not be realised. It would be a serious drain on resources. By 1960, 865 houses were owned by St Dunstan's estate and let to St Dunstaners and 107 widows, while mortgage schemes administered by the department also enabled many St Dunstaners to own their own homes.

Chapter 22

Physiotherapy – the Ideal Profession

'Go out into the sighted world – with your eyes wide open!'
(Llew Davies)

One area of employment made particular demands on Settlement Officer Peter Matthews and his staff after the Second World War. Finding premises in which a St Dunstaner working as a physiotherapist in private practise could combine as a family home and business with a suitable treatment room often proved a challenge. Massage or physiotherapy, as the profession had become known, was to become a very successful career for many St Dunstaners.

By the 1940s the course was much longer and, after a year of preliminary studies at St Dunstan's, candidates went on to spend two years at the Royal National Institute for the Blind School of Physiotherapy in London. During the worst of the bombing the student physiotherapists lived in Croxley House in Croxley Green, Hertfordshire and were driven to and from London in an army ambulance.

Bob Lloyd, whose adventures in Church Stretton as a pub-crawl guide appeared earlier, also had tales to tell of Croxley Green. He alleged that the house was haunted:

"One night I was awakened by a tugging on my bedclothes. I sat up but there was no-one there. I went to sleep only to be awakened shortly afterwards by the feeling that two hands were slowly moving up my legs and reaching up to my thighs. I sat up again and swung my arm as if to ward off anything that could be there. Again there

was nothing. The next morning I mentioned this incident expecting loud laughter. But much to my surprise my room-mate, Eric Foster piped up saying he had had a similar experience but kept it to himself.

"The next day an unpleasant odour permeated our room. Workmen inspected the chimney to see if it contained a dead bird but there was nothing. They pulled up the floor boards and found nothing. They replaced the boards and we never had that smell again and neither were we awakened by ghostly hands."

Local information was that Croxley House had been a convent in earlier years and Bob speculated "Scratched on the window near my bed was the date 1786. Could a nun have inscribed this to commemorate a special event in her life? Or perhaps something had been buried under the floor boards and it fell to us to release it. Who knows?"

These ghostly experiences did not hamper Bob Lloyd's and Eric Foster's studies, as they both became highly successful physiotherapists. Bob in private practice and Eric in the National Health Service. Totally blinded at the age of 23 in Tunisia, in 1946 Eric returned to Barnsley, his home town, after qualifying. His department was a small room in the town centre when he started, yet in 32 years service he had become District Physiotherapist, heading a staff of 25. He even designed his own physiotherapy department at Barnsley General Hospital, with a hydrotherapy pool.

Supervising a busy department and staff might seem impossible for a totally blind man, but Eric says he sees in his mind's eye: "I only have to put my hand on a patient and I can tell. I can also see if a physiotherapist is pleasant, happy, smiling or miserable. It isn't just the tone of voice, it's the pressure built up by antagonism, resentment, or, for instance, I can see if that person is smiling. I can see every move they make".

In 1937 one of Eric Foster's First World War predecessors used much the same words in describing his work as masseur to Everton Football Club. Harry Cook had played amateur football for Clitheroe and had had ambitions to play for Everton before being blinded. Speaking to a journalist about his 15 years with the famous Liverpool team, he said, "I don't have to wait for the voice to know who is my patient on the massage table. Small peculiarities in the limb tell me his identity at once. A slight thickness about the ankle tells me that 'Dixie' Dean is on the table. Charlie Gee has two scars on one knee where cartilages were removed. Tom Lawton has a longer tibia shin-bone than any of his club mates. Joe Mercer has a slight curve in his shin-bone. Albert Geldard – very hairy legs". Those who follow association football will recognise some names to conjure with among Harry Cook's patients.

The change of name from massage to physiotherapy was a recognition that modern techniques such as short wave diathermy, ultrasonic therapy and infra-red irradiation had changed the profession. These changes had begun between the wars when rudimentary electrical treatments were introduced: Faradism, using a surging current and Galvanism, passing a direct current through the body. It was essential that the blind masseur using electrical equipment should be able to read a milliammeter, or galvanometer. In the early years this was achieved through a gadget invented by Ian Fraser. In his workshop he devised a clamping device which enabled the delicate needle of the instrument to be felt by the masseur's finger.

The electrical equipment was often unreliable, but St Dunstaners were taught to apply these treatments by Dr Murray Levick, a pioneer in medical electricity, and former Medical Officer with Shackleton's Antarctic Expedition. However, the Chartered Society of Physiotherapy had introduced a standard curriculum for medical electricity that was impossible for a blind masseur to fulfil, bringing problems of professional status. Although Dr Levick gave the blind masseurs certificates to practise, it took many years for the RNIB and St Dunstan's to achieve professional recognition from the Chartered Society.

The next generation of masseurs or physiotherapists began to enter the profession. In 1950 there were 119 war-blinded physiotherapists in practise in the United Kingdom, 68 from the First World War and 51 from the Second. Two thirds were in private practice. The first man blinded in the Second World War to qualify was a member of the Scottish National Institute for the War-Blinded. Douglas Calder came to St Dunstan's for initial training in physiotherapy and continued at the Physiotherapy School at the RNIB. He soon became a member of the Council of the Chartered Society of Physiotherapy and in 1950 treated the women players at the International Tennis Championships at Wimbledon, while another St Dunstaner, Fitzwilliam Hume Crowe, treated the men. In 1957 Douglas was succeeded at Wimbledon by Fred Ripley, a St Dunstaner who had been in the prisoner of war camp at Kloster Haina.

The first woman to qualify was Barbara Bell, whose story has already been mentioned. Her physiotherapy training did not begin at Church Stretton with her male contemporaries. Barbara explained, "I was a female and things being the way they were in those days it wasn't considered 'quaite naice' for me to do physiology and anatomy and things with the men". At the time she qualified, the Hospital Committee in Ilkley decided that Coronation Hospital should have a physiotherapy department. Barbara got the job: "I started it and for about four years worked alone. I didn't find I had to impress people with my efficiency – I don't think I ever thought about it. For four years I was the only physiotherapist at the hospital. It was a voluntary hospital then and people belonged to contributory schemes which qualified them for treatment at the hospital. They wouldn't have got physiotherapy anywhere else so I suppose it was a question of going and having that Bell woman or lumping it so they came along".

She was joined later by another physiotherapist who worked mornings only, while Barbara worked in the afternoon. So she still worked single-handed and this suited her strong feelings of independence, "Because I am working on my own and not falling over other people's apparatus and losing things because someone else has taken them. I know exactly where everything is after I have got it organised and I can put my hand on it at a moment's notice". In a busy afternoon Barbara treated as many as 24 patients in eight cubicles equipped with short-wave machines, ultrasonics, traction apparatus, and wax baths. Her efficiency was laced with warmth and sympathy in her attentiveness towards her patients, many of whom came for afternoon treatments at some inconvenience to themselves to be sure of getting Miss Bell. Barbara is now retired and in residence at Ovingdean.

Among male blinded physiotherapists it is not surprising that many of them most enjoyed treating athletes and sportsmen. In their sighted days they had often been sportsmen themselves and treating athletes brought them close to sport. Assistant Superintendent of the Physiotherapy Department at Mayday Hospital, Croydon, Llewellyn 'Llew' Davies, explained the professional interest in treating athletic injuries: "This is where you get perfection. Here you get a good chance of studying anatomy at its best. You feel the muscle tone, you feel the nerves. When you come to put an electric machine on to an athlete he will react quicker than anyone else. Take Mel Blyth, if you put a machine on his leg and you turn it up for Faradism, for stimulating the muscle, gosh, you have only got to touch the switch and his muscles are away".

In turn, Mel Blyth, a former professional footballer, said of Llew, "I always like to come to him. He seems to find out what is wrong. If he says,

'You'll be alright to play', I know I will be. I suppose you could just say it is my confidence in him". In Wales, before he was blinded, Llew played rugby. He was the physiotherapist of London Welsh and of Streatham/Croydon rugby clubs, as well as Vice President.

Llew maintained that work in the National Health Service provided variety and great challenges:

"In the Intensive Care Unit people who are unconscious can have a chest condition – pneumonia can set in and the patient could die. We are sent in to do chest therapy. You have to turn them, twist them. It is your job to get the patient to cough up that stuff. This is not easy. You sometimes come across a young girl just about half conscious and you've got to make up your mind to do the best job you can. You're human, you've got daughters of your own, kids like this. Sometimes the sweat rolls off my brow and sometimes tears roll down my cheeks too. I'm not ashamed of it."

There was another advantage of hospital over private practice, Llew felt:

"Having trained a physiotherapist, St Dunstan's puts him as a private physiotherapist because some people say that a blind man is more effective in surroundings he knows. This I will grant without any shadow of doubt but I have done 25 years in my department and I am quite familiar with my surroundings. The mere fact you have got to leave the house, catch a bus and mix with the public tends to broaden your knowledge of life. I think it is educational to go out into the sighted world – with your eyes wide open."

Chapter 23

'Handy Andies': the Deaf and Blind

'Life in My Hands'
(The title of blind and deaf St Dunstaner Wally Thomas's book,
published in 1960)

For a few St Dunstaners, there were much more difficult challenges. They were the deaf and blind, or the 'Handy Andies' as they called themselves – an allusion to their only means of conversation. When it came to employment, despite their training and abilities in Braille and skills learned in the workshop at St Dunstan's, potential employers found their double disability a bar to engaging them.

In 1960, one of St Dunstan's 'Handy Andies', Wally Thomas, wrote a book – or rather spoke it into a tape recorder. The title, *Life in my Hands,* is well chosen, because for Wally and his comrades their only means of communication was through their sense of touch. The written word by Braille through their fingertips, and conversation through the deaf/blind manual tapped out on their hands. The vowels – A, E, I, O, U are represented by the five fingers while various logical signs on fingers and palm represent consonants. There is also an invention called the Arcaid, which works like a small portable typewriter, with the usual sighted keyboard. The sighted keys produce the Braille letters as raised pins on a keyboard on the other side of the machine. A Braille output on paper can also be produced should the deaf blind user wish to have a record of the conversation.

The first few chapters of *Life in my Hands* provide an insight into the fascination that can grip someone taking on the extremely dangerous task of disabling explosives. Wally describes the explosion that cost him his sight and hearing because he did not lose consciousness. What follows is an account of despair and survival through the skill of surgeons, through his family and through St Dunstan's. Wally spent his rehabilitation and training at Ovingdean, and learned assembly in the engineering workshop, while being re-introduced to sport and dancing in his spare time. Wally relates the problems of communication with a series of comic descriptions, which bring a smile, even a chuckle, to the reader and show how he came back to life.

Training completed, Wally received a letter from St Dunstan's to tell him that efforts to find employment for him had failed:

'Unemployable. It was an ugly son of a bitch that word. Worse, it had many synonyms – useless, idle, finished...I was trained in assembly and became efficient. Sixteen firms were approached on my behalf and their reactions varied. The feeblest was, "We can't speak to him, what would happen in the event of a fire?" The briefest was "We can't accept the responsibility of this man".

I was trained in handicrafts. My Braille reading was speeded up and developed under patient instruction. There was no suggestion of mine that St Dunstan's didn't consider fully and there were dozens of their own suggestions for me to choose from. But this man was too much of a responsibility!'

Wally overcame his despair by taking on commissions in his own workshop for a light engineering firm; and finding another use for his sense of touch by 'listening' to his small son singing by gently putting his hands on his throat. Later he used the same method, placing his hands on the guitar his son was playing. Wally lived a full life, enjoyed his children growing up and travelling abroad with his family.

The despair that Wally experienced must have been felt by the other St Dunstaners who were deaf and blind. How did they cope? Ron Ellis was one of Lord Normanby's pupils at Kloster Haina prisoner of war camp. In 1942 Ron's sight and hearing were damaged through disease as a prisoner before he reached Kloster Haina. Before he was repatriated he had become completely blind. Like Wally, despite his training Ron Ellis found that his former employers would not re-employ him. For a time he worked as a telephonist, but this was impossible when he became totally deaf, and so he found his way in the countryside. With St Dunstan's help, Ron took up poultry farming and had a small holding with a greenhouse and enjoyed the company of his friends.

Another 'Handy Andy', Edward 'Teddy' Mills of the Royal Air Force, did not come to St Dunstan's when he was blinded and deafened in 1916. He came for training in 1933, depressed by his deafness rather than his blindness. He took to poultry-keeping and gardening. A father of three, during the Second World War he helped to make shutters for the black-out and erected bunks and put floor boards in the family ARP shelter.

Like Edward Mills, George Fallowfield was another who arrived at St Dunstans long after he was blinded. Although wounded in 1918, George did not come to St Dunstan's until 1923, when he was referred by Moorfields Eye Hospital. He joined others awaiting training at West House in Brighton: "We all got there [Regent's Park] in January, 1924. I was keen to learn Braille and my teacher was Miss Stacey, but she was by no means confined to Braille. She played a big part in all the sports and was the first to take me down to the lake and into a boat".

George became a keen rower and was also involved in the walking races in Regent's Park, as well as long walks sometimes as far as Southend. Deafness still interposed with some activities: "I did not take part in any swimming contests. Deafness can prevent one indulging in some forms of sport and swimming is one. During walks escorts did not use the manual alphabet, they wrote in block capitals across my back! The most anxious time was when my cox was getting my boat in position for the start of a sculling race and giving me the tip to start which was a smack on my toes".

Training completed George continued his sporting activities competing for the London Club against other St Dunstan's sports clubs, in Birmingham, Brighton and Manchester. He made baskets for the Sales Department. Like Wally Thomas, he also enjoyed foreign travel. A revelation, perhaps, of how much can be experienced despite not seeing or hearing. George built up a library of a hundred Braille books, and found a rewarding hobby in making scale models of the boats he used to scull in. He was also an active supporter of Brighton and Hove Albion Football Club, attending matches with a sighted friend, who reported which player had the ball using, as ever, George's fingers. One of his hands was Brighton, the other the opponents. The five fingers were the forwards while other players were represented by positions on the palm of his hand – goalkeepers at the base.

'HANDY ANDIES': THE DEAF AND BLIND

These stories could be equalled by other 'Handy Andies' – each one a triumph over an enormously difficult handicap. They show the encouragement of training: reading through Braille and communication with others through the deaf blind manual. They show the healing effect of developing skills in hobbies like Meccano; playing cards or dominoes with friends; making jigsaw puzzles; gardening and countryside pursuits. They also show the determination needed to survive the problems of communication and interaction with others that deafness and blindness create.

Chapter 24

Research

'Never saying "it cannot be done".'
(Reputation of Norman French, former St Dunstan's Head of Research)

In 1943 Ian Fraser was becoming disturbed by the number of casualties coming to St Dunstan's who were blind and additionally handicapped by lost or damaged hands. Although the numbers were not large they were significantly higher than in the First World War. The use of explosives in booby traps and the advances in medical and surgical treatment meant that those wounded seriously survived the trauma of their injuries better.

In his memoir, *My Story of St Dunstan's,* Ian Fraser explains that he decided that what was needed was a 'technical man, keen and ingenious and inventive, who could turn his hand to anything'. His problem was that any likely engineer would be already engaged in war work of some kind. Fraser wrote: 'I was at a loss until I had the idea of going to the Hospital at Roehampton to see if I could find a wounded or slightly disabled man to come and work for us'. He was taken to a bed where the patient, a sergeant in the Royal Electrical and Mechanical Engineers, was surrounded by all kinds of articles needing repair that belonged to staff and other patients. Peter Nye was the patient. Needless to say that among the items on his improvised work bench was a number of watches. "Are you a watch-maker?" Fraser asked. "No, but I'm getting on all right with them", was the reply that secured Nye the job.

The St Dunstan's Research and Development Department was established with the appointment of Peter Nye in 1943. It would be Nye's responsibility to set up and equip the department. As there was no room at St Dunstan's Headquarters, the department was set up in the spare ground floor and basement of the Talking Books sound recording department, in

Hinde Street, just north of Oxford Street. In wartime machinery and tools were in short supply, and amongst the machinery initially purchased for the workshop were a lathe, which had been originally sent from America under lease-lend and a universal milling machine brought from Germany when the industries in the Ruhr were dismantled in 1918.

Peter Nye had already studied the problems of Alan Nichols, a double amputee of the First World War, to gain an understanding of the needs of double amputees. In addition he now spent a week living with one of the Second War St Dunstaners as valet-companion learning his problems and coming away with many ideas for gadgets. Although this would always be an important part of his new department's work there were increasing numbers of St Dunstaners finishing training and entering employment in open industry. It was soon evident that many needed specially devised tools and equipment to improve their efficiency as blind workers. In fact many of the most successful ideas were taken up by firms when it was realised that similar devices would improve productivity for all employees, blind or sighted.

To meet all the needs of new St Dunstaners and those finishing training and entering employment the staff had to increase and provide more specialist types of training. For instance an outworker, R. Spurgeon,was mainly based at Ovingdean teaching the use of the weaving looms developed at Hinde Street. Yet, perhaps the most interesting member of staff was Tommy Gaygan, the telephone operator who served both the Research and Development and the Sound Recording Departments. Tommy was blinded and lost both hands in North Africa when a booby trap exploded in an abandoned enemy vehicle. He operated a switchboard developed jointly by St Dunstan's and Post Office engineers.

This ingenious device incorporated a series of foot pedals – rather like those used by an organist – and a cabinet containing 40 push-buttons covered by metal contact guide plates. Tommy could make, receive and extend calls by operating the push-buttons with a metal probe and co-ordinated foot pedal movements. The metal probe was fitted into a leather fore-arm gauntlet and helped him keep a sense of direction and touch. It must have taken long training and much concentration to use the switchboard successfully but Tommy managed this and also 'proof-read' the long-play talking book recordings before they were included in the library. His hearty laughter was legendary and could be heard throughout the building.

Weaving looms were also developed for handless St Dunstaners.

Weaving was first regarded as a hobby occupation, but later in a few cases it was a remunerative occupation. The first loom was constructed in 1946. Like Tommy Gaygan's switchboard it made use of foot pedals. Levers, which could be operated by a forearm, controlled other operations even the changing of shuttles. The loom had to be set up by threading the twill but after this a handless operator could generally work unaided until he had completed about 60 yards of cloth. Important as the looms were to those who learned to operate them, their use did not persist for many years.

The work of the department fell into two main categories: aids for daily living – particularly for the doubly handicapped – and aids for those in employment either in open industry, in their own small businesses or in home workshops. In January 1947, a new man was taken on. His name was Norman French and he would serve St Dunstaners for nearly 40 years. French was the last man to join the workshop team. He was the last because as the years went on the pressure on the workshop eased as the number of new handicapped St Dunstaners and placements in industry lessened. It did not mean there was no work but it did mean that fewer workers were needed. Eventually, Peter Nye's only member of staff was Norman French.

In 1959 Peter Nye qualified as an Associate Member of the Institute of Mechanical Engineers and moved on to join Courtaulds research department in Coventry. He had given 16 years of skill and ingenuity to help alleviate St Dunstaners' problems, particularly those who had additional handicaps. Now French was to soldier on alone. The experience he had gained under Nye stood him in good stead. Like Peter Nye, he was inventive and at home with machinery and tools. Just as Nye began with a one-man department, French would continue alone, with an output of special tools and gadgets that he maintained through to his retirement. He was praised by St Dunstaners, as was Peter Nye, for always listening to suggestions, however outlandish, with the reply, "We will try that" and never saying "It cannot be done".

Where the doubly handicapped St Dunstaners were concerned it is important to realise that one idea did not necessarily serve all and individuals had individual needs. For example some home telephones were adapted with a raised metal guide around the dial to keep damaged fingers from slipping; another telephone had an enlarged disc with large holes corresponding to those on the original dial to accept an artificial thumb. Special adjustable stands held the handset for the handless, with foot pedals to engage and answer the telephone. The typewriter had also always been seen as an ideal means of written communication for St Dunstaners. Now variations of the typewriter adapted for Alan Nichols after the First World War were supplied to his fellow casualties from the Second. On a personal level, such things as spoons and forks, liquid and soap dispensers, brushes, towels, cigarette holders, cigarette lighters, and even a snuff dispenser were created.

The importance of a Braille watch to St Dunstaners has been stressed earlier. For the handless St Dunstaners something different was needed. One answer was the repeater pocket watch, which chimed the hours and minutes when the winder was depressed. The problem was that these watches were virtually antiques and not easy to obtain. In 1949 a friend from Tembani days came to the rescue. Princess Eugenie of Greece obtained five watches through the Greek embassy in Switzerland and held out hope for more.

For handless St Dunstaners who wished to run small businesses – mainly shops, although one, Bill Griffiths, successfully ran a road haulage business until nationalisation – machines to sort coins and give change were made. A handless tobacconist had his own machine to store and issue cigarettes. For St Dunstaners employed in industry the list of various tools and gadgets is too long to give here. Visits to factories were made with a St Dunstan's Industrial Visitor in the relevant area to assess problems. Specially made machines for winding coils for rotors in electric motors; jigs for assembly workers; adapted measuring devices giving audio output; devices like these were continually in demand and many times saved a job for a blind man.

* * * * *

A housewife is just as much in employment as anyone in business. Winnie Edwards was pregnant when she was blinded and lost her hands in a munitions explosion. From the start the Research Department was there to help, modifying feeding bottles so that she could use them. Before the days of automatic washing machines and disposable nappies a simple machine was modified to enable her to wash nappies, which she then hung out using her stumps, pegging them with her mouth. Winnie's courage and ingenuity helped her bring up a family and keep house using specially adapted domestic tools – many of them simple rings through which she could put her stumps and carry out tasks like using the vacuum cleaner.

Richard Brett became a carpenter despite his total blindness and lack of hands. Many of his tools, like Winnie's, had simple rings attached. Using them Richard could saw, plane and chisel. He also had an electrically-driven plane grinder to give him further independence of sighted help. He produced small items of furniture for local sale and for St Dunstan's Sales Department. To see him confidently feel with his stumps across his bench for the tool he required was to fear an accident. In fact he rarely cut himself – certainly no more than any sighted carpenter. Another ring device – but much larger – large enough in fact to hold a bowling wood enabled Richard to play green bowls. All kind of devices were tried before a simple ring just less in diameter than the wood was found to be ideal. The ring was attached to Richard's forearm gauntlet and he achieved great accuracy. An assistant was needed only to place the wood in the ring before he bowled.

A helper was also required to load another device for Richard, but this one was created for a more frivolous activity. Again this was attached to his gauntlet and consisted of a spring loaded holder for a dart. The action of extending the arm in throwing operated a lever-controlled trip mechanism that released the dart. There was adjustment to vary the trajectory of the dart, which was made before the start of a match. Richard would invariably draw a laugh from his sighted opponents as, when his dart was flying too high he would request that the light above the board be adjusted, "Because the light is in my eyes".

Devices for recreation brought other demands. Special holders for Braille playing cards and dominoes; foot controls for the handless to operate record players or talking book machines. Perhaps the most interesting was the development of the rifle range at Ovingdean. A 25-yard range was set up with a .22 rifle. This was mounted on a swivel stand and constrained to fire only in a five foot bullet trap area. The constriction provided the means to enable a blind man to take aim. It was a short metal tube or ring surrounding the rifle barrel just short of the muzzle. Both rifle and ring were wired to twin frequency oscillators This produced sounds that the marksman could hear in his headphones. The frequency of oscillators gave a low note in headphones worn by the blind marksman when he was centred and on target.

When preparing to shoot, the blind marksman would don the headphones with the rifle fixed in the central position so that he could hear the sound he would be seeking to aim for the bull. The rifle would be released and he had to find that sound again. The handless could pull the trigger by cable and there was a vibrating trigger for the deaf/blind to aim by touch. The rifle range opened in 1947 and at the time was the only one of its kind. Ian Fraser fired the first shot and scored a bull, while Sir Colin Fletcher, Chairman of the National Small-bore Rifle Association shot blindfolded and surprisingly – or perhaps not – also scored a bull.

Surely the most outlandish recreation among doubly handicapped St Dunstaners was that enjoyed by Wally Thomas, who was deaf and blind as a result of an explosion while working on bomb disposal in the Royal Air Force. Wally was given the opportunity to fly in a two-seater glider and soon formed the ambition to pilot the machine himself. This was to be under the guidance of a sighted instructor but the problem was communication with his deaf/blind pupil. How could he tell Wally in what direction to manoeuvre the glider? Norman French solved the problem by making a miniature joystick for the use of the instructor. He modified a helmet worn by Wally and fitted vibrators inside. They were arranged to the front, back and sides of Wally's head and were linked by wire to the instructor's joystick. When the instructor moved his stick to the left a vibration felt by Wally on his left meant move the control column to the left; on the back of his head meant ease the stick back and so on. Using this equipment Wally was able to keep his machine ascending in a thermal up current and even control it in landing.

One invention above all is praised by handless St Dunstaners. It is the Clos-o-mat, a toilet fitted with an automatic bidet to enable a handicapped user to wash and dry after use. This had been introduced into hospitals in Germany and a visit there convinced research staff that this would be an ideal solution for blind and handless St Dunstaners giving them privacy. After successful trial installations at Ovingdean and Headquarters a Clos-o-mat was installed in the homes of all doubly handicapped St Dunstaners who wanted it.

Employment, recreation, daily living – perhaps even survival for blind and handicapped men and women in a visual world was the aim of the Research Department. How well they succeeded can be seen in the successful and fulfilled lives of the many St Dunstaners who needed its help.

* * * * *

St Dunstan's constantly endeavoured to overcome the two major problems for blind people: independent mobility and access to the printed word. Ian Fraser wanted to apply the scientific advances made during the war to these ends. He was especially intrigued by the ability of radar to detect aircraft and ships and in 1944 he suggested that it might be used as a guiding device for blind people to detect obstacles and landmarks.

The result was the formation of a Scientific Committee at St Dunstan's in 1945, chaired by Professor Edgar Douglas Adrian. Professor Adrian was a physiologist who had worked on nerve injuries and shell shock in London and at the Connaught Military Hospital in Aldershot during the First World War. After the war he resumed his research and among his experiments was work on the eye, winning him the Nobel Prize in 1932. St Dunstan's was extremely fortunate to engage his interest in the sensory problems of blind people.

During the two decades following the Second World War, experimental work for St Dunstan's was carried out in Sussex University, The National Physical Laboratory, Nottingham University, and the Lanchester College of Technology, Coventry. Professor Adrian was succeeded by Air Commodore Dacre, then in 1961 by Dr A.M. Uttley, of the National Physical Laboratory. Fraser was either lucky, astute or both in finding once again just the right expert to chair his committee. Dr Uttley was at the time Superintendent of the Autonomics Division of the National Physical Laboratory. He had also worked at the Royal Radar Establishment, as Deputy Chief Scientific Officer. He was shortly to become Research Professor of Experimental Psychology at the University of Sussex, and had had a distinguished career in behavioural studies and biological engineering.

Fairly early on in the 1940s, the Scientific Committee had received the verdict by Professor R.L. Beurle that the wavelength of the radar beam made it difficult to detect small objects at close range and the bulkiness of the equipment needed ruled it out of consideration. The committee turned to the problem of reading print long before the development of computers with the ability to talk. Talking Books had already been proven to be of immense benefit. However, research continued into equipment for the individual blind person to enable them to read the newspaper and correspondence.

A reading machine called the Optophone had already been in existence since the First World War. Invented by Dr E.E. Fournier d'Albe, the Optophone made use of the properties of selenium, whose electrical resistance varies with the amount of light falling on it. The printed matter was laid face down and a beam of light scanned the paper from below, while the selenium cells were placed to receive reflected light from the page above. The electrical impulses generated by the light played a different musical note from each cell, which were heard by the reader in earphones. Needless to say reading by music was not easy and required a blind person with patience and an ear for music. A young woman named Mary Jameson tested the Optophone in 1917. Yet even after a year's practice Mary could read only one word a minute.

Improvements were made to the machine and Mary began to read meaningfully, although, she admitted "the signals were rather faint and I rarely achieved more than 25 words a minute". Mary soldiered on with the Optophone and also organised an annual fundraising event for St Dunstan's. The St Dunstan's Scientific Committee eventually took up the Optophone to see if electronics could improve performance. Photo-electric cells replaced selenium, giving clearer and louder signals. Mary's reading speed increased to 40 words per minute and she could use the Optophone to read typewritten correspondence.

Mary Jameson worked on for St Dunstan's, pursuing her dream until her death in 1980. However, only she and some two or three other blind people ever mastered the Optophone's musical code, or its 'warbling sounds', as Fraser put it. While the machine had come as far as it could go, its scanning system, designed all those years ago, surfaced again in a much more sophisticated machine in the 1960s called the Kurzweil.

St Dunstan's was not the only organisation searching for answers to the problems of blindness during the 1950s and 60s. There was a burst of activity internationally and especially in the United States. During this period there was a flowering of interest in sensory aids for blind people in many parts of the world. It was as if scientists and engineers suddenly became aware of the advances in technology that might be used for this purpose. St Dunstan's brought together many researchers at an International Conference on Sensory Aids for the Blind in 1966. Papers on mobility problems, aids to navigation, echo-location in man and bats, monaural and binaural aids to mobility and aids to reading print were presented and discussed. Papers on reading machines included one by Professor J.G. Linville and Dr J.C. Bliss of Stanford University. They were working on the Optacon, a system of optical recognition of type faces, which could be 'read' by feeling the outline of the letter in tiny vibrating pins. Their paper concluded: 'The authors anticipate that a small hand-held device which is simply rolled over the page being read is now within the range of possibility'.

Just as Mary Jameson had tested the Optophone, Candy Linville, the blind daughter of Professor Linville, tried out the Optacon. Candy and her father came to St Dunstan's in 1971 to demonstrate the device. As members of the Scientific Committee sat around the table Professor Linville asked if there was something Candy could read – a newspaper he suggested. *The Times* of that day was produced and to the surprise of all the listeners Candy confidently read the headline and opening story on the front page!

As a personal reading machine the Optacon was an immense improvement. It was about the size of a small cassette tape recorder of that time. Candy scanned the line of print in *The Times*, using a miniature television camera held in her right hand. The index finger of her left hand was placed in a groove on the front of the machine where she could detect the tactile image of each letter in tiny vibrating pins under her fingertip as the camera passed over it. There was no doubting Candy's success. She explained that she could recognise the pattern of sensations under her finger as whole words.

However, once again many blind persons were unable to develop this ability or, in some cases, even determine one by one the letters outlined by those vibrating pins. Nevertheless a significant minority were able to make use of it. Training courses were run at St Dunstan's jointly with the RNIB. The Optacon had the advantages of being portable and also presenting mathematical and other symbols. An eminent St Dunstaner, Professor Maurice Aldridge, made great use of the Optacon in his linguistic work. In his speciality of mathematical linguistics making semantic analysis of sentences, the Optacon enabled him to read symbols, which could not be read by other means. Professor Aldridge studied Anglo-Saxon, Gothic, Old German, Icelandic, French and Latin and became Professor of General Linguistics and Phonetics, heading his department at the University of Witswatersrand in South Africa. As a young man Professor Aldridge was blinded in a gunnery accident while serving in the Royal Navy. At St Dunstan's he began the studies that later earned him a scholarship to Oxford University and led to an impressive academic career.

The Kurzweil Reading Machine could be described as a forerunner of modern computers, able to scan printed material and turn it into synthesised speech. It consisted of a scanner, computer and keyboard. Like the old Optophone, printed matter was placed face down on a glass plate and a beam of light scanned each line. The images registered by a camera were then translated by a computer, which generated synthetic speech. Although the evaluation proved the value of the Kurzweil, its size and complexity meant that it was mainly used in libraries and colleges. Now the advent of talking computers has overtaken its usefulness.

A joint evaluation by St Dunstan's and the Royal National Institution for the Blind was set up in St Dunstan's headquarters. A wide variety of trainees came in, and among them a young, relatively new St Dunstaner, Ray Hazan (later President of Blind Veterans UK), who could sometimes be heard talking back to the Kurzweil. Blinded by a terrorist parcel bomb while on duty with the Anglian Regiment in Belfast, Ray became a master of the talking computer in his work for his blinded comrades.

* * * * *

The 1966 International Conference also heard several papers on mobility aids. Radar had proved unsuitable as a means of providing improved mobility for blind persons. Now the researchers turned to ultrasonics. Professor Leslie Kaye used this form of energy to detect obstacles or landmarks and their distance from the blind traveller by measuring the time it took for the signal to be reflected back from an object.

In confined spaces it was very effective. Broadcaster Cliff Michelmore, with only a short initial practice, used it to negotiate an obstacle course in a television studio while blindfolded. In real life, the slight difference in signal for a step down or kerb was very difficult to detect. In a crowded area the multiplicity of echoes confused the blind walker.

The ultrasonic torch could be used successfully but the verdict was that so much information given through sound inevitably slowed the walker's progress, emphasising the fact that the nerve fibres linking the eyes to the brain outnumber those linking the ears by some thousands. Nevertheless in later years there have been other developments using ultrasonics with spectacles or tactile output linked with a cane.

Dr Alfred Leonard's work on ultrasonics in the Department of Psychology, at Nottingham University led to him visiting the United States, where he was introduced to a simple yet effective aid to mobility – the long cane technique, at the Blind Rehabilitation Centre, Hines, Illinois. Dr Leonard came back enthused and persuaded St Dunstan's that here was an idea well worth pursuing. A St Dunstaner was sent out to America to study the technique and report. Walter Thornton, a champion of independent mobility, who was involved in the experiments with both the ultrasonic torch and the spectacles, was chosen and, like Dr Leonard, was greatly impressed. He explained that the technique involved the use of a lightweight cane considerably longer than the usual white walking stick.

Each one is tailor-made for the user to reach his breast bone when held vertically. Held in the hand with a grip like holding a pen, the cane is scanned across the body in rhythm with each stride. Because of its length, the walker checks ahead of each foot as each pace forward is taken. This device significantly increased confidence and with it speed of progress. The long cane technique has become a regular part of mobility training in courses run by blind organisations today.

While none of the projects described, with the honourable exception of the American long cane technique, was widely taken up. Nevertheless men of science across the world brought their expertise to bear on the problems of blindness and began a quest which still continues.

Conclusion

The Blind Leading
the Blind

S t Dunstan's post-war years were an outstanding example of the blind
leading the blind, especially through the participation of St Dunstaners
in the management of the charity. At one time St Dunstaners were in
charge of four departments, with 100 years of service between them.

When Richard Dufton, the St Dunstaner who became Chief Designer
with Miles Aircraft, took up his post at St Dunstan's in 1961, he joined a
team of specialist heads of departments all of whom were war-blinded. They
were G.P. 'Pat' Owens, Industrial Director, and Peter Matthews, Estate
Manager, whose work has already been described. In 1954 Robin Buckley
became Appeals Organiser, and later Public Relations Officer. He was a
regular officer in the Royal Navy and became a specialist in defusing enemy
explosive devices. While completing the dismantling of a bomb in an Italian
un-manned torpedo boat, he was blinded when the fuse exploded. For his
courage he was awarded the George Medal.

In the early 1970s, there were still over 400 First World War St
Dunstaners and about twice as many Second World War veterans. Sadly
Lord Fraser died unexpectedly in December 1974, bringing to an end his 53
years as chairman. His memorial service in Westminster Abbey brought St
Dunstaners from all over the country to London, just as they had gathered
for his predecessor Sir Arthur Pearson.

The post-war years, one could say, represent the high point in St
Dunstaners' service to their fellows. At the same time, although the numbers
of First War men were dwindling many of the Second War people were still
in active employment throughout the community. We must not forget the
third generation of St Dunstaners; those blinded in Northern Ireland, Korea,
the Falklands, Iraq and Afghanistan. Some of these people have served as
members of the council or as trustees. David Stuttard came to St Dunstan's

in 2003, when his sight failed after 40 years in the Territorial Army as a Captain in the Corps of Royal Engineers. David received the MBE for his work with his own charity drilling for fresh water in Africa with the help of the Royal Engineers.

Ray Hazan, who was blinded in Northern Ireland, became President of St Dunstan's, following a tradition that the president should be a St Dunstaner, established when Sir Mike Ansell succeeded Sir Neville Pearson in 1977. Ray's service with Royal Anglian Regiment took him to Belfast where, while on duty, he had the terrible misfortune to open a disguised parcel bomb. The explosion killed a colleague but Ray survived totally blind, severely deafened, and without his right hand. Despite these handicaps, or perhaps because of them, Ray led the way in the use of computers in St Dunstan's. He served the organisation as Public Relations Officer and, latterly until his retirement, liaised between his fellow St Dunstaners and staff at headquarters.

Ray Hazan and the other St Dunstaners in this story are not the only people warranting mention. They are a few among many. It is not too much to say that these 3,000 plus men and women were and are special. In overcoming their own disability they have set an example to a doubting world that there could be "Victory over Blindness", to use Sir Arthur Pearson's words. St Dunstan's success in rehabilitating so many was built on their patience, persistence, good spirits and comradeship.

Now St Dunstan's has a new name: Blind Veterans UK. In addition to its commitment to the war-blinded, who still come from campaigns in a troubled world, the charity has taken on a new task. It is working for the rehabilitation and welfare of the many ex-servicemen and women who are becoming blind through age and illness rather than acts of war. The legacy of the blinded of two world wars is there for them.

Acknowledgements

Robert Baker, Collections and Archives Officer at Blind Veterans UK –
for ever-ready help.

Catherine Goodier, Editor of the *Blind Veterans UK Review* – for
encouragement.

Jen Newby at Pen and Sword Books – for advice and expertise.

Roll of Honour

St Dunstaners and St Dunstan's employees
who appear within this book

St Dunstaners:
Elsie Aldred
Professor Maurice Aldridge
Michael Ansell
William Appleby
Max Ash
Thomas Ashe
Edwin 'Eddie' Baker
John Batchelor
Barbara Bell
David Bell
Alec Biggs
Sadie Black (later Stokes)
Walter Bowen
Wally Bowerman
Zofia Bregula
Richard Brett
Archie Brown
Robin Buckley
Billy Burnett
Douglas Calder
Allen Caldwell
Joe Carney
T.W. (Bill) Chamberlain
Albert Clewlow
Billy Clough
Major J.B. Cohen
Harry Cook
Harry 'Johnnie' Cope
Jimmy Crawford
Fitzwilliam Hume Crowe
Charles Daly

Joe Daly
Llewellyn 'Llew' Davies
Vi Delaney (née Formstone)
Les Dennis
Sid Doy
Nathaniel 'Drummer' Downs
Thomas Drummond
Richard Dufton
Charles Durkin
Winnie Edwards
Marian Elias
Jimmy Ellis
Ron Ellis
George Fallowfield
Robert Finch
Patrick F.C. Fleetwood
Dennis Fleisig
Eric Foster
Lord Ian Fraser
Ossy Gannon
Patrick Garrity
Tommy Gaygan
Rev. Howard Gibb
Elmer Glew
Rupert Graves
Bill Griffiths
Benny Hamilton
Tom Hart
Ray Hazan
Wilfred A. Helm
Charles Hill
Winston Holmes

ROLL OF HONOUR

Charles Kelk
George Killingbeck
Sidney Kitson
Esmond Knight
G.W. Lamb
John Lawson
Mary Lawson
Sylvia Lawson
Maureen Lees
Jimmy Legge
Bob Lloyd
Alf Lockhart
Tom Lukes
Sir Clutha Mackenzie
D. Maclean
Frederick Martin
Peter Matthews
Emily McClarnan
Patrick McGloin
Duncan Matheson McLean
Norman McLeod Steel
Thelma Meredith
Tommy Milligan
Edward 'Teddy' Mills
Alan Nichols
Reverend Michael Norman
Andrew Nugee
Gwen Obern
Bob Osborne
G. P. 'Pat' Owens
Doug Parmenter
Geoffrey Pemberton
Norman Perry
Agnes Peters
Harry Preedy
Brenda Rea (née Henderson)
Thomas Ap Rhys
Fred Ripley
Tommy Rogers
Herbert Scaife

Bill Shea
Jimmy Shepherd
Ray Sheriff
Blodwyn Simon
Bill Slade
Beryl Sleigh
Ron Smith
Sidney Smith
Clarence ('Bill') Stalham
Second Lieutenant Stephens
David Stuttard
Wally Thomas
Walter Thornton
Edmund Toft
Alexander Viets
Jack Vincent
Ronnie Vincent
Joe Walch
Fred Wareham
Leslie White
Percy White
Eileen Williams
Thomas Williams
Tom Wood
Jimmy Wright
Mary Wright
Bill Young

**Staff and volunteers at
St Dunstan's:**
William G. Askew
Mr Atkinson
Ethel W. Austin
Lawrie Austin
Colonel Eric Ball
Claude Bampton
I.W. Bankes-Williams
Harry Bennett
Colonel R.E. Bickerton
Lady Buckmaster

167

Amy Campbell
Bert Cattermole
Ellen Chadwick Bates
Lord Chaplin
Dr E. Chittenden Bridges
Joan Clement
Margaret Cox
R.C. Davenport
Miss Edwards
Irene Fraser (née Mace)
Norman French
Dr Arthur F. Gervis
Miss Gurner
Henry Hall
Miss Hensley
Mary Jameson
Ernest Kessell
Miss Knutford
M.B. Lancaster
Sir Arnold Lawson
Miss Morris
Ken Mountcastle
Laura Mullins
Oswald Phipps, Marquess of
  Normanby
Peter Nye

Natalie Opperman
Major Arthur Ormond
Dorothy Pain
Arthur Pearson
Lady Ethel Pearson
Neville Pearson
Matron Hester Pease
Miss Postlethwaite
Matron Power
Sir Washington Ranger
Doris Sawyer
Ruby Smith
Mrs Spender
R. Spurgeon
Avis Spurway
Grace Stacey (later Hollins)
Henry Stainsby
Ernest Stanford
Sister Steine
Miss Stirling
Matron Adelaide Thellusson
Bill Tovell
Charles Vintcent
Lillian Vintcent
Miss Went
George Zipfel

Bibliography

Ansell, Colonel Sir Mike, *Soldier On* (Peter Davies, 1973)

Dark, Sidney, *The Life of Sir Arthur Pearson* (Hodder & Stoughton, 1922)

Dunlop, E.E., *The War Diaries of Weary Dunlop* (Viking Books, 1986)

Fraser of Lonsdale, Lord, *My Story of St Dunstan's* (Harrap, 1961)

Griffiths, Bill, (with Hugh Popham) *Blind to Misfortune* (Pen & Sword Books Ltd, 1989)

Ireson, Peter, *Another Pair of Eyes – The Story of Guide Dogs in Britain* (Pelham Books, 1991)

Lawson, Arnold, *War Blindness at St Dunstan's* (Henry Frowde, 1922)

Purse, Ben, *The British Blind – A Revolution in Thought & Action* (Buck Bros. & Harding Ltd., 1928)

Thomas, Mary G., *The Royal National Institute for the Blind 1868-1956* (Royal National Institute for the Blind, 1957)

Thomas, Wally, *Life in my Hands* (Heinemann, 1960)

Wagg, Henry T., *A Chronological Survey of Work for the Blind* (Sir Isaac Pitman & Sons, 1932)

Index

INDEX

INDEX

Blind Veterans UK Today

Much has changed since Sir Arthur Pearson established an organisation to help soldiers who lost their sight during the First World War. Today, that organisation – now known as Blind Veterans UK – has developed and extended its work to help all former Armed Forces and National Service personnel, no matter where they served and no matter what caused their sight loss. But what has not changed is Blind Veterans UK's commitment to ensuring that anyone who served their country should receive the help and support they need to lead fulfilling lives despite their sight loss.

Today, Blind Veterans UK exists as a national charity that provides blind and vision-impaired Armed Forces and National Service veterans with lifelong support. This includes welfare support, rehabilitation, training, residential and respite care. Blind Veterans UK helps its beneficiaries – known as members – learn the skills and techniques they need to live more independently with sight loss. The nature of that help is determined by a member's specific need. It can range from helping members learn techniques for everyday tasks, like working out the correct money in a shop or getting a train, to adapting their home to ensure they can live safely and comfortably.

In addition to supporting blind veterans across the UK through home visits from a dedicated team of Welfare Officers, the organisation operates three centres for recreation, training and rehabilitation. These are situated in Brighton, Sheffield and Llandudno. The Brighton centre was established in 1938, when it was purpose built with members' needs in mind. Both the Sheffield and Llandudno centres were opened more recently, in 2005 and 2011 respectively, and include state-of-the-art facilities developed specifically for members.

Now entering its second century, Blind Veterans UK is continuing to grow and develop its work. In 2012, the organisation launched a major recruitment campaign, aimed at increasing the number of blind Armed Forces and National Service veterans it helps. Blind Veterans UK is driven by the belief that no one who has served our country should have to battle blindness alone.

All of the services Blind Veterans UK provides rely on donations from supporters. The organisation also depends on the contributions of its volunteers, who support Blind Veterans UK giving us their time and helping with a range of activities. You can find out more about Blind Veterans UK and its vital work today by visiting the organisation's website at **www.blindveterans.org.uk**.